CERULEAN

*Also by Drew Hayden Taylor*

* Published by Talonbooks

# CERULEAN BLUE

a comedy in two acts

DREW HAYDEN TAYLOR

Talonbooks

Talonbooks
278 East First Avenue, Vancouver, British Columbia, Canada v5T 1A6
www.talonbooks.com

First printing: 2015

Typeset in Arno
Printed and bound in Canada on 100% post-consumer recycled paper

Interior and cover design by Typesmith
Cover illustration by Lester Smolenski

Talonbooks acknowledges the financial support of the Canada Council for the Arts, the Government of Canada through the Canada Book Fund, and the Province of British Columbia through the British Columbia Arts Council and the Book Publishing Tax Credit.

Rights to produce *Cerulean Blue*, in whole or in part, in any medium by any group, amateur or professional, are retained by the author. Interested persons are requested to contact Janine Cheeseman, Aurora Artists Agency, 19 Wroxeter Avenue, Toronto, Ontario M4K 1J5; TEL.: (416) 463-4634; FAX: (416) 463-4889; EMAIL: aurora.artists@sympatico.ca.

The original music score for *Cerulean Blue* is also available. Contact the composer at TEL.: (416) 795-2536; EMAIL: andrewclemensmusic@gmail.com.

LIBRARY AND ARCHIVES CANADA CATALOGUING IN PUBLICATION

Taylor, Drew Hayden, 1962–, author
    Cerulean blue / Drew Hayden Taylor.

A play.
Issued in print and electronic formats.
ISBN 978-0-88922-952-5 (PBK.). – ISBN 978-0-88922-953-2 (EPUB)

    I. Title.

PS8589.A885C47 2015          C812'.54          C2015-904159-7
                                               C2015-904160-0

*To Ms Willie,*
*who keeps my world*
*from getting blue…*

# PLAYWRIGHT'S NOTE

Greetings and welcome. If you are expecting this play to be an exploration of some travesty of society visited upon the Aboriginal people of this country, or perhaps an examination of horrors or atrocities Native people have had to endure due to colonization ... you may be a little disappointed.

*Cerulean Blue*, like many of my previous plays, is a little more positive. I like to think of it as a celebration of the Aboriginal sense of humour. Yes, there are some issues thrown in here and there – after all, what's life without a few issues – but essentially, I have always felt the best medicine for many critical issues has always been a liberal dose of humour. That's what this book will attempt to do.

But first things first: a little background. This particular play is a bit of a departure for me. I and my work are known for dealing primarily with the Aboriginal community. And while a good chunk of this play takes place in a Native community, the vast majority of the central characters in this play are ... how should I put this ... colour challenged? Pigment denied? People of pallor? You get the picture.

In the spring of 2013, I was writer-in-residence in the Faculty of Arts at Ryerson University. In the nearby Ryerson Theatre School (which ironically are part of the Faculty of Communication and Design), there are two fabulous women. One is Peggy Shannon, chair of the theatre school, and the other is Cynthia Ashperger, the director of the actor's program, whom I'd had the opportunity to work with several times previously. Be that as it may, a number of interesting things happened during my residency and, just after my term ended, Peggy and Cynthia asked me to write a new play for the graduating class of RTS. I was excited but found the invitation a little daunting. You see, the graduating class consisted of twenty people, each of whom needed a role. In theatre, that's a lot of people wandering the stage. In Canadian theatre you're lucky if you can get a play with more than four characters produced; six if you are lucky and personally know the artistic director. I had never written a story with that many characters. The result is that some of the roles in *Cerulean Blue* are big and others are small, with barely a few lines; yet hopefully all are memorable and interesting. Of course, depending on the director and staging decisions, it is feasible the play could be produced with maybe fourteen or fifteen actors, doubling up some of the roles.

Another concern was that none of the actors in that year's acting program were Native. But what's a challenge without a little difficulty? Thus was born *Cerulean Blue*, the story of a blues band caught behind the lines at a Native protest. And let me say this upfront, seldom have I had so much fun working on such a project. The enthusiasm, the joy, and the dedication those students (and everybody involved) put into their effort, humbled me. And made me feel old.

In this play there's music, an all-out brawl, some romance, laughs, and lots of wacky characters. I hope you'll have as much fun with this play as I did. Thanks to the amazing Andrew Clemens for his fabulous music; he made my lyrics actually sound passable. Special thanks also to Cynthia, Peggy, and the amazing Ruth Madoc-Jones, who helmed the madness I helped create.

Special thanks to my editor, Ann-Marie Metten, and publisher, Kevin Williams, at Talonbooks, who somehow manage to keep me sounding coherent and somewhat reputable as a playwright.

– Drew Hayden Taylor

# PRODUCTION HISTORY

*Cerulean Blue* was commissioned for the Ryerson Theatre School and first performed at Abrams Studio Theatre in Toronto from February 5 to 12, 2014, with the following cast and crew:

RUSSELL: Drew O'Hara
CASEY: Taylor Hammond
ASHLEY: Mani Eusis
ANDY: Jake Vanderham
JOANNE: Zenna Davis-Jones
PAULINE: Vasilisa Atanakovic
BILLY: Owen Stahn
JENNIFER: Molly Reisman
ANGELA: Victoria Houser
HELENA: Caitlin Graham
OFFICER DELAIRE: Isaac Powrie
BUCK: Eddie Gheorghe
SADIE: Dion Karas
ARTHUR: Mena Massoud
LENORE: Emily Nixon
RUBY: Jade O'Keeffe
OTTER: Maaor Ziv
POCO: Zach Parkhurst
DAVE: Andrew Pimento
EMCEE: Kaleigh Gorka

Directed by Ruth Madoc-Jones
Musical direction by Andrew Clemens
Sound design by Gordon Walker
Set design by Holly Meyer-Dymny
Lighting design by Andrew Morris
Costume design by Sidney Toole
Production management by Isabella Cesario
Stage management by Seren Lannon

# CAST OF CHARACTERS

RUSSELL: Lead singer in the band
CASEY: Lead guitarist
ASHLEY: Keyboardist (Casey's wife)
ANDY: Drummer
JOANNE: Bass player
PAULINE: Russell's sister
BILLY: Joanne's replacement and Pauline's boyfriend
JENNIFER: New keyboardist
ANGELA: Band hopeful
HELENA: Ashley's mother
OFFICER DELAIRE: Police officer listening to the story
BUCK: Native bus driver
SADIE: Billy's old girlfriend
ARTHUR: Sadie's new boyfriend
LENORE: Festival organizer
RUBY: Festival organizer who is completely silent
OTTER: Ruby's translator
POCO: Barricade security
DAVE: Barricade security
EMCEE: Master of ceremonies at the Peterborough Blues Festival

# LOCATION

*Various locations in Toronto.*
*A bus.*
*And a First Nations campground in north-central Ontario.*

# TIME

*There's no time like the present.*

# ACT ONE

# SCENE ONE

*A police station. OFFICER DELAIRE sits at his desk, listening to BILLY and RUSSELL, who are seated across from him. OFFICER DELAIRE seems weary. BILLY and RUSSELL seem nervous and look a bit roughed up.*

OFFICER DELAIRE

Okay let me hear it one more time.

RUSSELL

Again?

BILLY

It's been twice.

OFFICER DELAIRE

Humour me. Three's the charm.

BILLY

Do you have anything to eat? We've been here like ... four or five hours. I need to be fed and watered every three hours or so. It's a Native thing. (*pause*) Seriously.

RUSSELL

It's true. Or he gets cranky.

BILLY

I do. Really.

OFFICER DELAIRE

Well I can get cranky too. And I have a Taser. A gun. And a pair of rubber gloves. So now tell me what happened again.

RUSSELL

Again. Well again, my name is Russell Aymes ... hi ... and this guy here is Billy Burroughs, and we're in a band.

BILLY

Not the local Native kind of band. He's talking about a musical band. Actually, I'm a member of both but ...

RUSSELL

We're called Cerulean Blue. A sort of avant-garde, progressive blues band. We sort of like to mix the traditional blues sound with more of an eclectic ...

OFFICER DELAIRE

Yes, I know. You've mentioned that. *Ad nauseam*. Get on with what led to the riot!

BILLY

I'd hardly call it a riot.

RUSSELL

More of an aggressive social interaction.

OFFICER DELAIRE

Aggressive social interactions seldom require two squad cars, a SWAT team, and two fire trucks. Remember the fire ...

RUSSELL

Ah yes, the fire ... That was not our fault.

OFFICER DELAIRE

So you say. Now I believe this all started at …

RUSSELL

We were at a wedding.

BILLY

Yes, a wedding.

OFFICER DELAIRE

Why do these things always start at weddings? Let's see … this was the wedding in Toronto …

## SCENE TWO

*Wedding reception. People are milling around. PAULINE and BILLY enter and sit together at a table near the back. HELENA, mother of the bride, approaches her daughter ASHLEY and gives her a big hug.*

HELENA

That was so beautiful. You were so beautiful. Everything was so beautiful.

ASHLEY

Yes, Mom.

HELENA

And Casey looked so handsome, didn't he?

ASHLEY

He did, Mom.

HELENA

I still think that dress shows too much cleavage.

ASHLEY

I know, Mom.

*ASHLEY spots her new husband, CASEY, walking to the front of the room where the band is set up. He waves to her, and she eagerly grabs the opportunity.*

ASHLEY

It's showtime, Mom.

HELENA

Seven years of piano lessons and this so-called band is what you have to show for it?!

ASHLEY

Yes it is, Mom. But think of it this way, I took six years of tap too. I could have become a stripper.

*ASHLEY leaves her mother, HELENA, and walks towards CASEY.*

HELENA

Ah sweetheart, I know, but you're still young.

*ASHLEY joins CASEY onstage. They kiss.*

ASHLEY

Thank you. If I didn't love you before …

CASEY

I could see you were in trouble so it was either this or pull the fire alarm. You have a peculiar relationship with your mother …

ASHLEY

Everybody has a peculiar relationship with their mother. Mine
is just more obvious. In the world of migraines, she's what's
called a "carrier."

*JOANNE joins them.*

JOANNE

Last show, guys ... How does it feel? After this, you're
civilians again.

CASEY

Bittersweet. It will be weird for sure, having no more band.
No more endless hours of rehearsal. No more arguing with
Russell about all his rules. I hope he's cheered up a bit.
He seemed to take our getting married so personally. I am
going to miss all of you – Ashley will too – but there is life
beyond this band. All our planets are aligned and all the signs
say "move on." And who are we to argue with fate?

ASHLEY

Or reality. You know, last month I made $223 as a member of
Cerulean Blue – $223!

JOANNE

We all made $223 last month. All things considered, it was a
good month.

CASEY

The crack addict down our street makes more than that.
And he doesn't have to chip in for gas when we have a gig
out of town.

ASHLEY

Joanne, look. You know we're gonna miss hanging out with
you and Andy and Russell. But you have that cushy part-time
job at Baskin Robbins to get you through the hard times. Ice

cream pays your rent. We don't have any ice cream. We're lucky if we've even got ice.

CASEY

There's more waiting for us out there in the big world than just the band. This wedding ... everything ... It's a new beginning for us. The possibilities for our future are endless.

ASHLEY

More importantly, if I stay with Cerulean Blue, that means I have to keep staying at my mother's ...

CASEY

... *we'll* have to keep staying at your mother's ...

ASHLEY

And if that happens, frankly, $223 a month won't cover the meds I'll end up having to take.

CASEY

The meds *we'll* end up having to take.

JOANNE

Ah yes, "Better mental health through family relocation." I know it well. That's why I left Sudbury. I'll miss you two. ( *pause* ) So where's our fearless leader?

CASEY

Haven't seen him since the ceremony. He's probably still moping.

JOANNE

Well, with you two leaving, you're practically cutting the band in half. And while I do, as you say, have my treasured position as assistant manager at Baskin Robbins, and you two have each other, Cerulean Blue is all he has.

ASHLEY

Maybe he's grabbing a smoke out back with Andy?

JOANNE

He quit smoking two months ago, remember?

*ANDY walks by.*

JOANNE

Hey Andy, have you seen Russell?

ANDY

(*rhyming*)

*Ah Russell Aymes, I know not where he is.*
*Maybe he's in the washroom, taking a whiz.*

CASEY

Why the hell did Russell make our drummer the lyricist?

JOANNE

He listens to too much Rush. (*spots RUSSELL putting away his cellphone*) There he is. (*yelling*) Russell! (*RUSSELL approaches*) You know we were supposed to go on twenty minutes ago?! This is for Ashley and Casey's wedding?! Where were you?

RUSSELL

Putting out fires. Belleville and Oshawa just cancelled. And I think the Barrie festival is a little shaky too. I managed to salvage Guelph and Peterborough. Thank God for university towns.

JOANNE

What's up with Belleville and Oshawa?

RUSSELL

> The blues aren't as popular as they used to be. Everybody wants hip hop or hard rock these days. ( *to ASHLEY and CASEY* ) One last time, sure I can't talk you out of it? Cerulean Blue just won't be the same without you. I might be able to up your per diem ...

CASEY

> We got a per diem?

ASHLEY

> A case of beer is not per diem. Sorry, Russell, but it's time for us to move on. We've got plans. There's a new life ahead of us. You know I'm going back to school and Casey ... he's got a job as an apprentice chef.

CASEY

> I'm gonna make sauces.

RUSSELL

> A *new* life?! Cerulean Blue *is* life.

ASHLEY

> It's *your* life, Russell. And it seems to work for you. But this doesn't have to be difficult. We'll be around. Give us a call if you need us but we've outgrown the garage-band phase of our life. It happens to most people. But we'd like to go out with a bang.

RUSSELL

> We are not a garage band! We are an artistic endeavour full of innovation and invention. I will not have you slander Cerulean Blue. But I do not bear grudges. Let's rock ... or as the case may be, let's blue. Where's Andy then?

JOANNE

> That's him over there, hitting on Ashley's mother.

RUSSELL

Probably trying to figure out what rhymes with MILF.
(*yelling*) ANDY! It's showtime!

*They all take their positions on the stage. ANDY sees them and
quickly runs up to the drum kit. RUSSELL takes the mike.*

RUSSELL

Everyone, welcome to our final show, as the band was born.
But while we shall mourn the passing of what once was, this
is in fact an evening of celebration. So this is for the happy
couple. The true heart and soul of Cerulean Blue.

*They play an original song.*

(*singing*)

I'm tired of walking and I'm tired of talking.
I'm tired of crying and I'm tired of dying.
I just wanna get through this last dark night.
I'm tired of chasing and I'm tired of freebasing.
I'm tired of hiding and I'm tired of sliding.
I just wanna win this one last battle.

(*chorus*)

Sometimes you lose sight when you realize the road
is too long.
Just close your eyes and walk forward.
What's behind you doesn't matter.
Though it's like standing up front, forgetting words
to your song.

*Near the back of the hall, PAULINE and BILLY get up and dance.
RUSSELL notices this and watches for a moment, wondering
who is dancing with his sister.*

(*singing*)

*I'm tired of fighting wars and I'm tired of sleeping
    with whores.*
*I'm tired of choosing and I'm tired of losing.*
*I just wanna feel something again.*
*I am tired of crying and I'm tired of lying.*
*I am tired of bleeding and I'm tired of needing.*
*I just want to belong somewhere.*

> ( *chorus* )

*Sometimes you lose sight when you realize the road
    is too long.*
*Just close your eyes and walk forward.*
*What's behind you doesn't matter.*
*Even though it's like standing up front, forgetting
    the words to your song.*

*Once the song is over, they all bow to the applause, then turn
and hug each other. It is the final performance of Cerulean Blue,
as it started.*

HELENA

What a charming song for my daughter's wedding.

*The band members go their separate ways in the reception, and
RUSSELL puts away his guitar.*

ANDY

> ( *rhyming* )

*Hey man, what a great way to end the night.*
*And you, my friend, don't give up the fight.*

RUSSELL ·

Give it a rest, Andy. It's not cute anymore.

ANDY

> (*rhyming*)

> *I don't know what you mean...*
> *jellybean.*

> *ANDY moves off and starts tearing down his drum kit.*

RUSSELL

> (*to himself*) I've got to stop listening to Rush.

> *PAULINE approaches him while BILLY gets them a drink.*

PAULINE

> Hey.

RUSSELL

> Four years of political science at Queens and that's the best
> you can do.

PAULINE

> Hey... you? I can say that in Chinese, French, Spanish, and
> Hindi, big brother.

RUSSELL

> Glad you could make it to the wedding. And did you notice we
> didn't throw rice, as per your suggestion? Or confetti.

PAULINE

> Yes, that was very noble of all of you. Every little bit helps,
> whether it's saving the pigeons or the trees. There may be hope
> for you yet.

RUSSELL

> Who was your friend?

PAULINE

Somebody new.

RUSSELL

A new boyfriend. Okay, let's see. He's not handicapped.
Doesn't appear to have been recently beaten up by the police.
Doesn't look like a migrant farm worker or textile worker. Is he
a defrocked gay priest with Tourette's syndrome?

PAULINE

Why do you always mock me?

RUSSELL

Because, little sister, you are very mockable. Your last boyfriend
was a black Haitian transsexual. And he was the most
normal. I can't make this kind of thing up. Conformity is not
your thing.

PAULINE

He was not my boyfriend. The transition to becoming a man
can be difficult. I was just helping him. Sexually.

RUSSELL

Mom and Dad would be so proud.

PAULINE

You liked him.

RUSSELL

Yes, I did. And so did you, then he got a job at a bank.
Discovered Hugo Boss and bought a Honda Civic. Oddly
enough, he became less interesting for you ... What do
you have against Honda Civics? So again, what's this guy's
dysfunction?

PAULINE

He doesn't have any dysfunctions.

*BILLY approaches them and hands PAULINE a drink.*

BILLY

Here you go. Wow, drinks are expensive here. Back on the reserve, it's usually an open bar at weddings.

RUSSELL

Ah, First Nations. Hi, I'm Russell, Pauline's brother.

BILLY

(*shaking hands*) Yeah, cool. Billy. You're pretty good up there.

RUSSELL

Thanks. We try.

PAULINE

So what are you gonna do now? I mean with Casey and Ashley gone.

RUSSELL

Regroup I guess. Once the dust settles. Find replacements. Hold auditions. That kind of thing. I'll have to scour all the restaurants and Second Cups for out-of-work musicians. I hate doing that. All these baristas with big puppy-dog eyes ... That's why I don't drink coffee anymore.

PAULINE

Well, Billy here plays guitar.

RUSSELL

Oh he does, does he?

BILLY

> I do. And a little singing too. Pretty good if I do say so myself.

RUSSELL

> How convenient. What a coincidence eh, Pauline?

> *PAULINE shrugs.*

RUSSELL

> So what do you know about the blues?

BILLY

> It can be kind of depressing. Just like your song. You ever listen
> to any of those old-time blues artists? Man, you can tell they
> had it rough. And I thought we Aboriginals had it tough. I used
> to think they should have called it the "reds" instead of the
> "blues." (*laughs*)

RUSSELL

> Yes, very funny. Thanks for the keen insight.

BILLY

> I do what I can. Anyway, what's a nice white boy like you doing
> playing the blues? Get a flat tire one morning? Your *Globe and
> Mail* subscription run out?

> *Now it's PAULINE's turn to laugh.*

RUSSELL

> That's ... amusing. I'm truly amused. The mystique behind
> the blues sound goes beyond colour, beyond socio-economic
> history, it's a pan-racial cry of acknowledged injustice that sees
> no boundaries ...

BILLY

> I'm sure that's exactly what Robert Johnson would say.

PAULINE

Billy honey, another drink please.

BILLY

I think I can arrange that.

*BILLY exits the scene.*

RUSSELL

I don't like him.

PAULINE

You don't like anybody who challenges you. But he's good ...

RUSSELL

You want him in my band! Is that what this is about?

PAULINE

You don't have a band anymore. You have half a band. You need a guitarist. I have a guitarist. That's more than a coincidence. That's divine intervention.

RUSSELL

Cerulean Blue needs more than just a guitarist. Our music is eclectic and sublime. It's subtle, yet overpowering at the same time. It needs those with a skilled touch ...

PAULINE

Billy has a skilled touch. You don't even know how good he is.

RUSSELL

It's more than that. With every First Nations person I have ever met, it's usually either AC/DC or country. Or AC/DC country. Cerulean Blue is neither.

PAULINE

That's racist.

RUSSELL

Listening to AC/DC is racist?!

PAULINE

It won't hurt to try. Give him a chance.

RUSSELL

What's the point?

PAULINE

Give him a chance.

RUSSELL

Is this one of your "make-work" projects?

PAULINE

Give him a chance.

RUSSELL

But I don't like him.

PAULINE

Give him a chance.

*Both are silent for a moment.*

RUSSELL

Fine. Okay. Sure. I'll give him a chance. I don't know why.
We have to hold auditions anyway. But if I don't like him ...

PAULINE

You will.

*PAULINE walks away and joins BILLY.*

RUSSELL

Son of a bitch, I hate her. Hey Andy, ready to hold some
auditions this weekend?

ANDY

(*rhyming*)

*Cerulean Blue will not die an easy death.*
*I know that what was lost to love shall be found again.*
*Let me know when and where you want me, my brother.*
*Ashley and Casey's end shall be somebody else's begin-... ning.*

(*pause*) I'll work on it.

## SCENE THREE

*Audition room, early afternoon. JOANNE, ANDY, and RUSSELL
are sitting along one side of a table. In front of them is a young
woman, ANGELA, auditioning with keyboards/guitar etc. She is
playing a pretty bad version of the opening riff of "Smoke on
the Water." After a particularly bad flourish at the end, she stops,
pleased with her work.*

ANGELA

Ta da! I know I sound a little rusty but I promise you I can get
better. Practice makes perfect you know. The ten-thousand
hour rule and all. I'm only at a couple hundred hours right
now but the sky's the limit. I've got a long weekend coming up
to add on a couple dozen hours. So what do you think? Do I
gotta chance?

*All three are quiet, equally uncomfortable at answering her
question.*

RUSSELL

Uh, how familiar are you with the blues?

ANGELA

I saw the *Blues Brothers* movie. And the sequel.

RUSSELL

I see.

JOANNE

Would this be your first time playing in a professional band?

ANGELA

Yes, it would be but I have to be upfront about this.
I understand you do some engagements outside of the city.
I'm not sure how feasible that is with my current schedule.
My manager at the Second Cup is quite a stickler about
shift changing.

RUSSELL

Does anybody have any other questions?

ANDY

(*rhyming*)

*Nope, I'm good.*
*I know what I should.*

RUSSELL

We'll be in touch. Thank you.

ANGELA

No. Thank you! Really, I mean it.

*ANGELA packs up her stuff and leaves.*

RUSSELL

Maybe we can break Ashley and Casey up. What do
you think?!

*ANGELA sticks her head back in the room.*

ANGELA

Uh sorry. One final question. You see, I turn twenty-seven in October and I've got concerns about that musical Twenty-Seven Club? You know, the one where everybody dies. Do you have any sort of health benefits?

RUSSELL

No, I'm sorry.

ANGELA

You should look into it. Talk to you soon. Bye.

*She exits once more.*

ANDY

(*rhyming*)

*Joanne and Russell, I'm sad, man, really sad.*
*To tell you the truth, they're all exquisitely bad.*

JOANNE

So who's next? Some refugee from a grade-six ukulele class?

RUSSELL

Well, this should be interesting. My sister's boyfriend.

JOANNE

Is that the tall, Spanish-looking guy?

RUSSELL

He's not Spanish. Native. Ojibway, I think. And he's got attitude. Not the fun kind.

ANDY

(*rhyming*)

*Well, let's see him play those funky frets,*
*And maybe get us some cheap cigarettes.*

JOANNE

> ( *looking at ANDY* ) And to think you have a master's in Can Lit.

ANDY

> Yes, I do.

>    ( *rhyming* )

> *I know my Margaret Laurence, Robertson Davies,*
>    *Stephen Leacock, and my Al Purdy.*
> *I know my Leon Rooke, Catharine Parr Traill, Wayson Choy,*
>    *and my Susanna Moodie.*

> *I know my Alice Munro, Marian Engel, Miriam Toews, and*
>    *my Lucy Maud Montgomery.*
> *I know my Rudy Wiebe, Farley Mowat, Sinclair Ross, and my*
>    *M. G. Vassanji.*

> *I know my Jane Urquhart, Margaret Atwood, Leonard Cohen,*
>    *and my Michael Ondaatje.*
> *I know my Morley Callaghan, Tom King, Mordecai Richler,*
>    *and my Dennis "fucking" Lee.*

> Question?

JOANNE

> None whatsoever.

> *RUSSELL gets up and opens the door, ushering BILLY in. BILLY
> carries his guitar.*

RUSSELL

> Everyone, this is Billy ... Uh, Billy ...

BILLY

> Billy Bison.

JOANNE

> You're kidding?!

BILLY

Actually yeah, I am. People kind of expect names like that from
Native people. My real name is Billy Burroughs but I always
thought Billy Bison would be a cool stage name. "Appearing
one night only, Billy Bison and the Lost Tribe!" I'm told half of
being successful is being memorable.

ANDY

(rhyming)

*I like him already,*
*Freddie.*

BILLY

Wow, you're all white. Playing the blues. Wow, talk about your
shift in cultural perception. Shouldn't it be a sort of a baby-blue
or pale-blue colour instead of cerulean blue ... ?

JOANNE

Excuse me, I'm not white. I'm Irish. We faced quite a bit of
racism ourselves, you know. All that potato-famine stuff. And
my great-grand uncle's wife knew people in the IRA.

BILLY

I'll alert Amnesty International.

JOANNE

I see what you mean.

BILLY

Sorry. My fault completely. I haven't had lunch yet and I have
a filtering problem. Comes from growing up with four sisters
and five brothers. You learn to be fast and cut to the bone,
or you'll be trampled over and forgotten. The Elder on my
reserve suggests I be a sniper rifle instead of a shotgun. You
know, be selective instead of taking shots at everybody. Wise in
his own way. He's a cool Elder, if a little gun happy. Look, I'm
here to audition ... can I still?

ANDY

> ( *rhyming* )

No problem, my friend, show us what you can do.
There might be a home for Billy in Cerulean Blue.

BILLY

> Thank you … member of Cerulean Blue …

>> ( *pulls out his guitar; then begins to play and sing along* )

>> You play and party with all of your friends. Not me.
>> You keep telling me you don't like being alone.
>> You always say you miss me and want me around.
>> But you never pick up when I telephone.

>>> ( *chorus* )

>>> You are who you are and I can't change that.
>>> I'm me. I'm me.
>>> You're the woman I want. Not some copycat.

>> I want to take you places and show you things. With me.
>> Time to share all of our tears and laughter.
>> I can only wait so long before I say goodbye.
>> Start a new book by ending this chapter.

>>> ( *chorus* )

>>> You are who you are and I can't change that.
>>> I'm me. I'm me.
>>> You're the woman I want. Not some copycat.
>>> I'm me. I'm free.
>>> Maybe you're not the woman I want. Just some
>>> copycat.

*The song is not quite the blues but close enough. As he plays, it becomes evident that he knows how to handle the guitar and can even sing. ANDY and JOANNE are impressed. RUSSELL, though, still doesn't like BILLY.*

BILLY

(*finishing his song*)

That's just a little something I wrote on the bus, the first time I came to Toronto. I know, it's kind of weird, but so is love.

JOANNE

I see you're not exactly unfamiliar with a guitar.

BILLY

You know, I had a whole mess of siblings but the guitar was my only real friend. I could talk to it and it could talk back.

ANDY

(*rhyming*)

*Now that sounds so bluesy.*
*And we aren't in a position to be choosy.*

Russell?

RUSSELL

Billy, thank you. Can I have a word with my friends for a moment?

BILLY

Hey, it's your band.

*BILLY gathers up his stuff and exits.*

RUSSELL

(*to BILLY*) Yes, it is. (*to the others*) I say we keep looking.

JOANNE

Why? He's the best we've come across so far who doesn't smell like espresso.

RUSSELL

We should look some more. There's got to be lots of guitarists out there. We've only scratched the surface. Besides, you heard him. I think he's racist against white people.

ANDY

(*rhyming*)

*Is that possible? Can Native people be racist?*
*Now that's a thought-provoking topic of interest.*

JOANNE

Yeah, that's kind of annoying. But he did apologize. And he's good. Andy likes him. I like him. Your sister likes him. Russell …

RUSSELL

I still don't like him.

JOANNE

Let's put it to a vote then. The remaining three members of Cerulean Blue. All those in favour of accepting Billy Bison – I mean Burroughs – into the band, raise your hand.

*ANDY and JOANNE each raise their hand.*

JOANNE

Two. All those not in favour?

*RUSSELL raises his hand.*

JOANNE

That makes one. The ayes have it.

RUSSELL

Hey, this is my band. When did it become a democracy?

JOANNE

Good question. Let's see. It stopped being a dictatorship
when we started and still do use my father's van to move our
equipment. Your tight control also weakens every time we
practise in Andy's basement. The fact Casey used to arrange
most of our bookings also looks suspiciously like democracy.
And Ashley, well, her mother would give us a forty percent
discount at her store when we needed sharp clothes to
perform in. It seems your entire contribution to our collective
is the name Cerulean Blue and playing the guitar. And some
songwriting that our buddy here seems to help you with.
Do you get where we're going with this, Russell?

RUSSELL

That's … that's … that's a little unfair. I birthed Cerulean
Blue. I weaned her. I held her hand and taught her to
walk and … And if I do say so myself, I am the heart of
Cerulean Blue!

JOANNE

Hearts can be transplanted. Yes, Billy's a little obnoxious. But
Andy and I are used to that. Happens in some creative types.

ANDY

( *rhyming* )

*That's like the pot calling the kettle black,*
*You tell him, sister, you give him the facts.*

RUSSELL

We still have to find another keyboardist.

JOANNE

( *looking at clipboard* ) The last four people all play keyboards.
How convenient. Russell, would you be so kind as to let
Jennifer Redfield in? And don't pout. Makes you look twelve
years old.

*RUSSELL opens the door and an incredibly perky JENNIFER bounces in.*

RUSSELL

I'm not pouting. I am registering disapproval.
Jennifer Redfield?

JENNIFER

Me! Me! That's me. Where do you want me to go?

JOANNE

By the keyboards might be a good idea.

JENNIFER

I should tell you right off the bat. I'm a born-again Christian.
I hope that's not going to be a problem. Don't worry, I won't
get all in-your-face about it.

ANDY

(*rhyming*)

*She believes in the Father, Son, and Holy Ghost.*
*Great! For I too am a fan of the Host of Hosts.*

JOANNE

I'll give you twenty bucks or a bucket of butterscotch ice cream
to stop doing that …

JENNIFER

Does anybody here have a favourite hymn, or should I just do
the Beatles?

JOANNE/RUSSELL

(*shouting*) BEATLES!

# SCENE FOUR

*Rehearsal room. Deserted. Then the door opens and JOANNE,
ANDY, and RUSSELL enter, carrying their equipment. They look
around. It's obvious most of them have never been there before.*

JOANNE

> Wow, this is nice. A real rehearsal hall. How did you
> pull this off?

RUSSELL

> Your comment about not really being a good leader and always
> rehearsing in Andy's basement kind of hurt. So I decided to be
> more proactive and arranged this.

JENNIFER

> (*entering*) Okay. Everybody make yourself comfortable. I want
> everybody to feel at home.

JOANNE

> Oh, it's hers.

RUSSELL

> I am just maximizing all the assets currently available to us.

ANDY

> (*rhyming*)

> *Hey Russell, how about I set up my drums back there in the rear?*
> *With the shape of the room, that's probably the best place to hear.*

> *For the rest of the scene, ANDY is setting up his drum kit,*
> *occasionally leaving and returning with various components.*
> *JOANNE helps.*

JOANNE

> (*to JENNIFER*) How did you get this place?

JENNIFER

My roommate, Melinda, is an installation artist. And a missionary. But for the next two months she's going to be in Guatemala teaching the local indigenous population how to do installation art. Isn't that fabulous?!

JOANNE

Yes, installation art, that's so much more important than literacy or proper medical care. So you share this place with her?

JENNIFER

Yeah. The Lord has been kind to us.

RUSSELL

( *to JOANNE* ) It's still better than Andy's basement. No spiders, or stains of questionable or scary origins.

ANDY

( *rhyming* )

*Watch it my friend, my couch, I defend its glory,*
*Because every stain has its own sweet story.*

JOANNE

Ick.

*Sound of a knock at the door; then BILLY and PAULINE enter.*

BILLY

Ah, this *is* the right place. Hello ... this house!

PAULINE

It's certainly big enough. Hey everyone, I think you all know Billy?

JOANNE

I don't think Jennifer does. Jennifer, this is our new guitarist, Billy Burroughs. This is Jennifer Redfield.

JENNIFER

Oh wow, I am so glad to meet you. Isn't this exciting!

BILLY

I guess it must be. You certainly are enthusiastic!

JENNIFER

I know! Why not be?! This is such an adventure. Prior to this, I'd only ever played in church choirs or with my family. I tried busking once but people can be so rude.

*JOANNE leans over to speak privately with ANDY.*

JOANNE

(*whispering*) When we do our coffee run, she only gets decaffeinated.

JENNIFER

(*to BILLY*) And where are you from?

BILLY

I'm from a small Ojibway reserve northeast of here, a place called Otter Lake.

JENNIFER

Oh my. Let me say, I am personally sorry for all the sorrows and tragedy individuals in the Church inflicted upon your people. Those residential schools and things. It was so ... so ... sad.

BILLY

Yes, it was. On behalf of all the First Nations people in Canada, let me say ... thank you and I hereby absolve you of all blame and responsibility. Go in peace. And this is Pauline, my girlfriend.

RUSSELL

And *my* sister.

PAULINE

Also an individual in her own right. But hello anyway, Jennifer.

JENNIFER

Hi. Love your boots.

RUSSELL

I think this is already a bad idea.

PAULINE

You being pessimistic again?

RUSSELL

Sounds like the beginning of a joke. "This Native guy and a Christian join a blues band ..."

ANDY

(*rhyming*)

*No, no, my friend, this is gonna be fun,*
*Provided she doesn't turn into a nun ...*

If you know what I mean.

RUSSELL

Andy, no. You know the rules. No inter-band fraternization.

JOANNE

We will not go through that again. It does not have a good history.

ANDY

(*rhyming*)

*Did you tell that to our friends Casey and Ashley?*
*You were never comfortable as their relationship grew*
*    anatomically.*

RUSSELL

And look what it caused us. No sinning with the Christian!

*ANDY is not pleased.*

ANDY

(*rhyming*)

*Russell is a big fat meanie,*
*Who didn't know what to do with his own little weenie.*

RUSSELL

Hey!

JOANNE

Don't look at me. I never said a thing.

*PAULINE approaches.*

PAULINE

I heard you gave Billy a rough time at the audition.

RUSSELL

What are *you* doing here?

PAULINE

I'm here to watch. Make sure you boys are playing nicely.

RUSSELL

Sorry, but we have a rule. No boyfriends or girlfriends allowed at rehearsal.

PAULINE

Ah yes, your famed "Yoko" rule.

RUSSELL

It's not my rule. We all agreed on it.

PAULINE

Joanne, did you agree with Russell's "Yoko" rule?

JOANNE

Hell no. I hate how the woman is always blamed for things like that.

PAULINE

Andy?

ANDY

(*rhyming*)

*Personally I think Yoko's work is too much maligned.*
*And I believe in the need for rules, but sorry, bro, not that kind.*

PAULINE

There you go. Mind if I sit over there?

RUSSELL

If I answered that, would you listen?

PAULINE

(*preoccupied with helping BILLY*) Sorry. Listen ... ?

RUSSELL

Yep, good to have you home.

BILLY

(*to PAULINE*) I am having second thoughts about this. I'm already getting nervous.

PAULINE

You'll do fine. I promise.

BILLY

How can you promise something like that?! This is completely out of your control. It's me with the problem.

PAULINE

Trust me. I'm white. We know these things.

*This manages to get a smile out of BILLY.*

PAULINE

Now that's the smile I fell in love with. We'll do this together.

RUSSELL

( *now ignoring his sister* ) Okay, listen up everybody. This is the first rehearsal of what I guess you could call Cerulean Blue 2.0. But first things first, I'd like to welcome Jennifer and Billy to our little group. To quote the immortal words of Ronny Hawkins, "You won't make a lot of money but you'll get laid a lot."

*The women are oddly enough not impressed by this kind of endorsement. RUSSELL's joke falls flat.*

RUSSELL

So much for breaking the ice. Does anybody have anything to say before we rehearse?

JENNIFER

I do. First of all, I want to thank you all for letting me into your family. This really means a lot to me. I just hope I can measure up. I've said a prayer for all of us. And I made cookies.

ANDY

( *rhyming* )

*Ooh, I like her already. Look at those yummies.*
*These are my favourite, except for fudge brownies.*

RUSSELL

Oh good. Now I guess we should ...

BILLY

Can I say something? I'd just like to thank everyone for this
opportunity. I brought along some sweet grass. I thought it
might be a good beginning if we ... maybe ... had a smudge
ceremony or something. It might ... calm us down ...

JENNIFER

A smudge ceremony. What's that?

BILLY

It's like a purification ritual. It cleanses your mind, body, and
spirit. We use it to begin meetings, ceremonies, anything
personal and official. It's a great way of focusing.

RUSSELL

( *to PAULINE* ) Is he for real?! A purification ritual?! We're a
rough-and-ready blues band. We don't purify.

PAULINE

You usually take two showers a day and only drink filtered
water. At least you used to.

RUSSELL

That's different.

PAULINE

With you, it's always different. It was always your toys. Your car.
Your way of doing laundry ...

RUSSELL

Is this the fabric-softener issue again? I told you ...

PAULINE

Sounds like its "your band" too. See, it's a pattern. If it doesn't
fit into your little world, it's wrong.

*JOANNE overhears part of this.*

JOANNE

Yeah, had to always sleep on the side of the bed nearest the bathroom. Always put up a fuss if he couldn't. Do you know he wears his shirts and pants sequentially? He has to wear everything once before he'll rewear something. Drives him nuts to go out of sequence.

RUSSELL

You had three-year-old blouses and dresses in your closet that still had the price tag on them. Where's the sense in that? I'm just egalitarian!

JOANNE

With clothes? That's not egalitarian. That's just weird. Is there a reason we're discussing Russell's peculiarities, or just for fun?

PAULINE

Just a reality check.

JOANNE

I think you're twenty years too late. I think Russell is half French and half OCD. Do you know about the dishwasher? He freaks out if you don't let him stack the plates.

RUSSELL

That's because you do it all wrong. You have to let the water ...

BILLY

(*to ANDY*) What the heck did I start?

ANDY

(*rhyming*)

*Trust me, it's a long story with lots of pain.*
*If you ask them about it, it will drive you insane.*

BILLY

Maybe I'll save the smudging ceremony for a later date.

*BILLY suddenly gets a call on his cell. He discreetly tries to take it.*

JOANNE

Back to the present, Andy's kit is set up. How do you
want to do this, Mr. If-It's-Thursday-I'm-Wearing-
the-Powder-Blue-Shirt?

RUSSELL

Okay, so I gave Jennifer and Billy written copies and recordings
of our set list late last week, to familiarize themselves with our
sound and what I like to call our "edge." Jennifer, do you have
any questions?

JENNIFER

No, sir. I have familiarized myself with most of your lineup.
Some very sophisticated material here. I've always had a
fondness for minor keys. I just hope I can keep up.

RUSSELL

So do I. Now, Billy, as lead guitarist, you will of course be
primarily responsible ... ( *noticing BILLY is on the phone* ) Excuse
me! Billy!

*BILLY puts up his hand telling RUSSELL to wait a second.*

RUSSELL

( *astounded* ) Did he just give me the hand?! He can't give me
the hand! This is his first day. And we have a firm no-cell rule
in the rehearsal room. Billy! Are you or are you not part of this
band? You are keeping us waiting. Pauline ... ?

*PAULINE goes to BILLY, who nods, hangs up the phone, then
whispers something to PAULINE, who gets equally excited.*

ANDY

> ( *rhyming* )
> Looks like Billy got some pretty good news.
> That's usually counterproductive when you're playing the blues.

RUSSELL

> I bet Ringo didn't keep the other boys waiting while he talked on his cell.

JOANNE

> No cells in the sixties, genius. And Ringo was the drummer, not the lead guitarist.

RUSSELL

> Must you always correct me?

JOANNE

> Russell, if I didn't always correct you, you'd still think people put K-Y Jelly on their toast.

RUSSELL

> You have a long and evil memory.

> *PAULINE and BILLY approach.*

PAULINE

> Hey, we got good news for the band!

RUSSELL

> We'll be the judge of that.

BILLY

> I've got us a gig.

RUSSELL

> You got us a gig?! Hey, *I* get the gigs. *You* can't get us gigs. You haven't even started the first day of rehearsal yet. How can you get us a gig?

PAULINE

Seems Billy did.

JOANNE

Let him talk, Russell.

RUSSELL

Did you not hear me talk about the gig-making hierarchy in this band?

JOANNE

Ah yes, Russell's I-arrange-the-gigs rule. You've got us four in the next seven weeks. I think we can fit in one or two more, if we use a crowbar. Billy, tell us what's going on.

BILLY

Are you all familiar with what's happening up at Dead Rat River?

RUSSELL

Did you say "Dead Rat River"? What the hell is a Dead Rat River?

PAULINE

Let him finish. Billy ... ?

BILLY

It's a First Nations community up north.

JOANNE

And why is it called Dead Rat River?

BILLY

Somebody probably found a dead rat in the river ... probably a muskrat actually.

JENNIFER

So they called it Dead Rat River after that? That sounds kind of … nasty. "Hi, I'm from Dead Rat River." Doesn't exactly roll off the tongue.

BILLY

You have to understand how things used to work a hundred years ago. White people would come into communities and meet people whose names they couldn't pronounce. So often they would just make up names to make their lives easier. My last name is Burroughs. Not exactly the most Aboriginal of names. Dead Rat River is what white people called the place. It's Anishinabe name is actually Gizhi Waawaabagonoojibon.

JOANNE

Wow. That's a mouthful. What does it mean in English?

BILLY

Dead Rat River … Anyway, anybody here familiar with what's going on up there … ?

RUSSELL

… in Dead Rat River …

BILLY

That's the place.

ANDY

(*rhyming*)

*Wait a minute. Wait a minute. That place has been in the news. People are fighting. Some big politician proposed a truce.*

BILLY

Yes. Big land issues. Aboriginal rights. Logging rights. Mining rights. All that sort of fun stuff.

RUSSELL

And where does Cerulean Blue come into this?

BILLY

There's a big fundraising event happening up there at the end of this week, to help the community. Anybody who's anybody is going to be there. There's talk of Blue Rodeo being there, Sarah McLachlan, Bruce Cockburn, and maybe even Buffy Sainte-Marie ...

JENNIFER

Ooohh, I loved *An Officer and a Gentleman*.

JOANNE

What?

JENNIFER

"Up Where We Belong." She co-wrote the theme song for the movie.

BILLY

Among a few other things. Anyway, I know some people who know some people, who owed money to other people. Knowing I was going to be a part of this band and had to pull my weight, I made a few calls, talked to a few people. I know I probably exceeded my authority as the new guy but I knew things were happening very quickly up there and I had to act fast. So I got us an invitation to the music festival!

PAULINE

Isn't that great?!

*The other members of the band don't know how to react.*

JOANNE

Wow. Cerulean Blue at Dead Rat River. One night only. I don't think we know any Robbie Robertson tunes.

ANDY

    (*rhyming*)

*I am all for new experiences, man.*
*But this has got to be a new one for the band.*

RUSSELL

    Okay. And just how much does a fundraising concert at
    Dead Rat River pay?!

BILLY

    Oh. Well … you see … the thing is … maybe I should have put
    more emphasis on the word "fundraiser."

JOANNE

    Oh shit.

ANDY

    (*rhyming*)

*I read in the papers that it's kind of far away from here.*
*What is it, a four-hour drive to where we're close, or at least near?*

BILLY

    More like five.

PAULINE

    You're all missing the point. Think of the cause … and … and
    this is an excellent opportunity to be a part of something
    big and important. It's good karma. There's more to life than
    just money …

RUSSELL

    There's more to life than just food but it's kind of difficult to get
    through the week without some. (*to JOANNE*) You see, this is
    why *I* book the gigs.

PAULINE

> Think of it, guys. What an opportunity! Blue Rodeo. Buffy
> Sainte-Marie. Bruce Cockburn ... when are you going to get
> a chance to hang out and play with a lineup like that. You're
> thinking short term. Look at the long term. Could make some
> interesting contacts. I'm sure one or two of their agents might
> be there. The press sure will be. This could be the biggest thing
> you've ever been a part of. This is something you should be
> thanking Billy for.

> *Once more the band looks a little uncertain, but they are begin-
> ning to buy into Pauline's persuasive argument.*

RUSSELL

> Pauline, nice try ...

BILLY

> It's catered. All the fresh fish you can eat.

JOANNE

> Oh, I like fresh fish. Actually, Russell, it could be
> interesting ... All that press wouldn't hurt, I suppose. God
> knows we could use the exposure.

JENNIFER

> Yes, He does.

ANDY

>     *( rhyming )*

> *Yeah, Dead Rat River ... It does sound kind of exotic*
> *But five hours north, that's just short of the Arctic.*

JOANNE

> Yes, Andy, there is life outside of Queen West. Jennifer, now
> that you're a member of Cerulean Blue, what do you think?

JENNIFER

Thank you for asking. That's so sweet. Well, I think it's a good idea. Like Pauline says, it's for a good cause. We must support our fellow band member. Yes, there's no money involved, but the best and most important things usually aren't paid. Think of it ... think of it like missionary work.

BILLY

Please don't talk like that up there.

JOANNE

Russell ...

RUSSELL

Now you're asking me what I think?

JOANNE

I told you, don't whine. Ruins the blues-band image. Muddy Waters never whined.

RUSSELL

Where will we stay? How will we get there?

BILLY

No problem. They said they'll put us up. And they said they might be able to arrange travel if we need it.

PAULINE

Don't be a pain in the ass, Russell.

RUSSELL

(*indicating PAULINE*) I think that position is taken. I say no. It's too far away. No money. Don't know the area. We'll get lost among all the big-name draws. It's too much of a wild card. And we won't have had enough rehearsal time. Too soon.

JOANNE

> Okay. Time for another vote, I guess. Who does *not* want to go to Dead Rat River?

> *RUSSELL raises his hand. He is alone.*

JOANNE

> Okay, who does want to go to Dead Rat River?

> *One by one, everybody but RUSSELL puts their hands up.*

JOANNE

> There you go. Democracy rules again. All hail the voice of the people. Rage against the machine and all that. Dead Rat River, get ready to welcome Cerulean Blue.

ANDY

> (*rhyming*)

> *Democracy can and often is a double-edged sword, my friend. Helpful one minute, the next you'll find it up your rear end.*

PAULINE

> This is all good, guys! I'm sure you'll love the experience.

JOANNE

> As long as we're only gone a few days. I have to be back at work by Monday for the launch of this new line of Asian-flavoured ice cream that Baskin and Robbins is introducing. Supposed to be the hit of the summer. Sushi and Kimchi.

JENNIFER

> This is so exciting. What does one wear to a First Nations political protest?

BILLY

> Guilt.

# SCENE FIVE

*Cerulean Blue is waiting on a street corner. Bored and annoyed.*
*Except for ANDY, who is sound asleep amid the equipment.*
*BILLY and PAULINE are stacking luggage.*

PAULINE

You okay?

BILLY

A little anxious. This band thing ... I think I may have bitten off more than I can chew. And you've seen me eat.

PAULINE

Things will be fine. And I'm getting tired of telling you that. At some point, you'll have to believe me.

BILLY

Too much too soon. We should just cancel Dead Rat River. Baby steps. Not a good place to lose your virginity.

PAULINE

Calm down. Take a deep breath. Things will happen as they will happen. And I'm sure people have been losing their virginity in Dead Rat River for generations.

BILLY

Very funny. I was speaking metaphorically.

PAULINE

I'm not. You don't have to be afraid. Normally, there's a purpose to fear, and your particular fear has no purpose.

BILLY

Does anything scare you?

PAULINE

Poverty. Injustice. Ignorance. Racism.

BILLY

Oh those.

*RUSSELL approaches.*

RUSSELL

They're late.

BILLY

( *to PAULINE* ) Was he born this cranky?

PAULINE

Nobody else is getting upset. And it's only been half an hour.

RUSSELL

It's about respect. We're professionals. *We* expect to get treated like professionals. If they say they are going to pick us up at 10:00 a.m., then I expect them to pick us up at 10:00 a.m. You know, Andy, getting up before noon goes against nature.

PAULINE

I'm sure he'll survive.

RUSSELL

He's a drummer. He can survive on coffee, cigarettes, and cold Egg McMuffins. I had a nightmare once, the end of the world came and went, and the only things to survive the destruction were cockroaches, Tim Hortons, and drummers.

*He shivers. Suddenly, a rundown school bus shows up. It pulls up in front of the band and the door opens. Sitting in the driver's seat is an older Native guy. His name is BUCK and a ripped piece paper he is trying to read.*

BUCK

Hey, I'm looking for some people called ... Kawartha Zoo?

RUSSELL

You mean, Cerulean Blue.

BUCK

Sure, why not. I'm here to pick you up and take you back to
Dead Rat River. My name is Buck.

JOANNE

Buck what?

BUCK

Just Buck. What's a matter? Buck not good enough for you?
You need one of those fancy Toronto last names?

JOANNE

No, that's fine. Buck is just fine. Just fine ... Russell ...?

RUSSELL

You were supposed to be here at 10:00.

BUCK

So you gonna call the bus-driving police? You're not the
Kawartha Zoo I have written down here, so that makes me
what you call flexible. The ways I see it, it's 10:00 somewhere in
the world. Now I didn't spend the last five hours driving here
just to get my ass chewed off. You coming back up north with
me or what?

JENNIFER

You wouldn't want to take a break first?! Grab some coffee or
breakfast? Five hours is a long time to do anything.

BUCK

What's with all the questions? I ain't getting paid to answer all these questions. Are you coming aboard or what?

RUSSELL

This is a school bus.

BUCK

Yesterday, it was a school bus. Tomorrow it will be a school bus again. Today it is a yellow multi-seated limousine for the Silly Two ...

RUSSELL

Cerulean Blue.

BUCK

I have yet to be convinced. So what are you gonna do?

RUSSELL

Okay, okay, hold your horses ...

BUCK

Hold my horses ... was that some sort of racist comment about me being Native?

RUSSELL

No! No, not at all. I just meant ...

BUCK

Then hurry up. I'd like to get home before the shooting starts.

JOANNE

What shooting?

BUCK

You do know you're going to a protest? A dispute with lots of cops and lots of Native people, and lots of disagreeing perspectives on the issue.

JOANNE

Billy, nobody said anything about any shooting.

BILLY

He's joking. I'm sure he's joking. Let's just load up.

PAULINE

(*to BILLY*) He *is* joking, right?

BILLY

There's a good chance. Um, Buck, are you gonna help us with all this equipment?

BUCK

See this right foot, lost three toes back in February of '04.

JENNIFER

Oh dear.

BUCK

Yep, wife hacked them clean off with an axe. A dispute over doing the dishes. You'll have to load all those things yourself. Now hurry before you make me irritable.

*They all start moving around and loading up the bus. Except ANDY.*

RUSSELL

Charming. You've got some interesting people up there in Dead Rat River.

BILLY

Not my people. I'm from Otter Lake, remember. I'm sure he's just one of the local colourful characters.

RUSSELL

I've got another bad feeling about this. See what happens with democracy?

JOANNE

Hey, who's going to wake up Andy?

*They keep loading but there is silence.*

JENNIFER

Would you like me to?

JOANNE

Yeah. Kick him if you have to.

JENNIFER

I will do no such thing. He seems like a sweetheart.

*With a smile, she walks towards ANDY. The rest stop loading, just for a moment, to watch. JENNIFER approaches the sleeping figure.*

JENNIFER

Good morning, Mr. Sleepyhead. Time to wake up! There's a whole new glorious day ahead of us. Wakey-wakey! ( *no response* ) Silly boy, we have to go.

*She touches him and he rolls over slowly and reacts sleepily.*

ANDY

( *rhyming* )

*Take me. I'm yours*
*Here amidst these sidewalk stores.*

JENNIFER

( *aloud* ) He said for me to take him. That he's mine.

JOANNE

Do you want to take him?

JENNIFER

Not really. I have a cat.

JOANNE

Then, if he tries to hump your leg, turn the water hose on him and he'll leave you alone. (*yelling*) Andy, we're leaving, load your stuff.

ANDY

(*rhyming*)

*Oh man. I had this horrible dream about our trip.*
*That we were going deep into the bowels of northern Canada.*
*Mosquitos and sasquatches and blackflies and ticks.*
*As nightmares go, it's almost as bad as getting a very cold enema.*

RUSSELL

No dream. Time to suffer for your art.

*Reluctantly ANDY gets up and starts loading his equipment onto the bus. BILLY goes up to BUCK.*

BILLY

*Ahnee,* I'm Billy Burroughs and I'm from Otter Lake.

BUCK

I'm so sorry. Are we just about ready to go, Billy Burroughs from Otter Lake?

BILLY

Almost. I've never been to Dead Rat River. Nobody in the band has either.

PAULINE

What's it like?

BUCK

Well, picture Toronto without all the buildings, streets, people, pollution, cars, lampposts, hookers, Starbucks, urban Indians, music bands, and attitude, and you're pretty close.

RUSSELL

I think everything's packed away.

BUCK

Then all aboard. Next stop, Dead Rat River.

*The band boards the bus and BUCK starts it up. He drives. Everybody settles in. ANDY goes back to sleep.*

JENNIFER

Mr. Buck, how long till we get there?

BUCK

If the highway gods are with us, four and a half hours. If not ... dawn. So what are you all going up to Dead Rat River for?

RUSSELL

They didn't tell you?

BUCK

Me? I just drive the bus. To me it's a good day if I let off as many kids in the afternoon as I picked up in the morning. (*beat*) You guys doing a wedding or something? Hope you know your country music.

RUSSELL

Actually no to both, thank God. There's going to be a fundraising concert up there and we've been invited to play. Some very prestigious bands are scheduled for the lineup. Blue Rodeo, Sarah McLachlan, Bruce ...

BUCK

Oh that. That was cancelled.

JOANNE

What?

BUCK

Cancelled. Negated. Null and void. Bye-bye.

RUSSELL

You're joking.

BUCK

As you might notice, I don't have much of a sense of humour.

ANDY

(*rhyming*)

*Cancelled?! Did I hear that correctly? What's off?*
*Has the reason for our trip to Hell been miraculously lost?*

RUSSELL

Calm down, Andy. Please tell us, why was the fundraising concert cancelled?

BUCK

Most of those fancy music people were a little uncomfortable being so close to all that trouble.

JENNIFER

Trouble? Oh my ... that can't be good.

BILLY

What trouble?

BUCK

Geez, don't they tell you guys anything? The land dispute. The
province and the municipalities are disagreeing somewhat
strongly with the feds and the DRR band council. Police are
all over the place. Big Native people with big guns. Actually,
lots of guns. Angry people of all colours. Ways of lives being
threatened. Corporations smelling money. So, seems the
people putting this thing together couldn't get what-d'you-
call-it ... insurance ... to bring all these big-time people in to
play. So one by one, they went bye-bye. You guys, however,
are the only ones left. Guess you weren't high enough in the
pecking order to warrant insurance. Pretty cool, huh? You've
got the whole event to yourselves ... not that too many people
will be able to get in. Sure you don't know any country music?

PAULINE

Oh shit.

BUCK

Don't get your moccasins in a knot. It's very unlikely people
will start shooting. Last three games of the playoffs are
this week.

RUSSELL

( *to BILLY* ) Billy Burroughs, what the hell did you get us into?

BILLY

I ... I ... it sounded good ...

PAULINE

Russell, don't yell at him. He didn't know.

BUCK

Billy ... Billy Burroughs ... Yeah, I thought that was the name.
I got a message for you.

BILLY

Me? What message? From who?

BUCK

A woman came up to me just as I was pulling out. I think her name is Sadie. And the message ... what was the message ... oh yeah: "Come here and you're dead." Something like that.

*Unfortunately, BILLY recognizes the name.*

BILLY

Sadie ...? Sadie Thompson?! She's up there?

BUCK

Sadie Thompson, that's her full name. Yeah, she's shacked up with the chief for the last year. Don't think she likes you.

PAULINE

And who the hell is Sadie Thompson?

BILLY

An ex-girlfriend, from a couple years back.

BUCK

Yeah, runs the DRR equivalent of the Warrior Society up there.

RUSSELL

Oh shit.

JOANNE

Double shit.

JENNIFER

Oh pooh.

PAULINE

Is this the one you told me about …

BILLY

Yes.

PAULINE

Oh shit. (*pause*) No insurance, huh?

# SCENE SIX

*Still on the bus, driving through central Ontario. Most are lost in their own thoughts, except BILLY and PAULINE.*

BILLY

(*whispering*) Pauline, maybe this is for the best. Maybe this is a sign from the gods. Maybe this was meant to be. Or not to be.

PAULINE

That is the question. Billy, you're just looking for an excuse.

BILLY

Like an alcoholic looking for vanilla extract, yeah! I never wanted to do this, Pauline. You know how uncomfortable it makes me. Extremely uncomfortable, and yet you made me do it. And look what's happening. Protests, blockades, cancelled appearances, weapons, ex-girlfriends. Weapons and ex-girlfriends, not a good combination. Did you ever think that maybe I am the way I am for a reason? And you shouldn't mess with the way God created me?

PAULINE

First of all, I don't believe in God …

JENNIFER

    I heard that.

PAULINE

    And second, we create ourselves. If there's one thing I learned
    in India ...

BILLY

    How to make an Indian's life miserable?

    *RUSSELL notices the momentum of the bus has changed.*

RUSSELL

    Hey, why is the bus slowing down?

BUCK

    Reason it out, Genius, we're almost there.

ANDY

    (*rhyming*)

    *Oh bliss, oh happiness, I can't believe we're finally here.*
    *My kingdom, the drummer cried, my kingdom for a beer.*

JOANNE

    Who are all those people up there?

BUCK

    That's the barricades. We have to get their permission enter.

JENNIFER

    Why do all those men look so mean?

BUCK

    No porta-potties here. This is where things get decided, people.
    It could mean we go ahead, or turn around and head back
    to Toronto.

ANDY

Oh fuck no. I hate buses. I hate buses. I don't care if it doesn't rhyme. I hate buses.

BUCK

Everyone smile.

*Everyone does.*

BUCK

I was joking. It won't help.

*BUCK opens the school bus doors and two men in camouflage ( DAVE and POCO ) come on board. They look very no-nonsense.*

BUCK

Dave.

DAVE

Buck. Okay. Who's in charge here?

*Everybody points to RUSSELL.*

RUSSELL

Oh sure, now I'm in charge. Yes, I'm Russell Aymes. We're Cerulean Blue. The band that's supposed to play tomorrow.

DAVE

*( to the other guy, POCO )* I thought that was cancelled?

POCO

No, just the good bands. Cerulean Blue ... never heard of you.

RUSSELL

Well, we're sort of an heterogeneous and interpretive take on the traditional urban blues sound. We try to incorporate ...

JOANNE

Russell, shut up.

DAVE

A band, huh? ( *approaching RUSSELL* ) You want to know something …

RUSSELL

That depends.

DAVE

I used to be in a band.

POCO

Oh God, not this again.

DAVE

Yeah, yeah, really.

RUSSELL

Oh … that's interesting.

DAVE

It was, I guess, what you would call a boys' band. Just a few years back.

JENNIFER

A Native boys' band … I don't know if that's funny or sad.

POCO

Dave, this isn't the time or the place.

DAVE

We used to be called New Kids on the Rez. Ever hear of us?

RUSSELL

Of course you were. No, I can't say that I have.

DAVE

We had one relatively big hit on all the reserve radio stations.
It was called ...

POCO

You're embarrassing me, Dave.

DAVE

Maybe you heard of it. "Baby, baby, I want to stick my totem
pole in your teepee."

BILLY

That was you? That was my sister's wedding-dance song.

DAVE

Testify!

RUSSELL

I can't say that I am familiar with ...

DAVE

Wait here, I got a couple of boxes of CDs back in the camp.
Be right back.

*DAVE runs out, excited.*

POCO

I hate it when he does this. ( *to the band* ) Okay, my mother
always taught me to be nice to strangers. So go. Run.
Hide. Quickly.

RUSSELL

We can go through here then?

POCO

Yeah. Sure. Go already! You're probably the last to get through though. I got word we're locking down the roads.

JOANNE

If you do that, how are people going to get in to hear us?

POCO

That's a very interesting question. But not my responsibility. ( *looking out the window* ) Oh, I see Dave coming. He's carrying his boom box too. I can't listen to that song again. Not anymore. He plays it ... And plays it ... Last time at a party he put it on, I woke up three days later in Timmins. Nobody deserves that. Run!

*POCO quickly evacuates the bus.*

RUSSELL

Buck, if you ...

BUCK

Way ahead of you. Dave's my nephew and every fucking family gathering ...

*BUCK floors it and everybody lurches backward as the bus picks up speed.*

BUCK

Just another half hour or so. God, this reminds me of my old demolition-derby days.

JENNIFER

Though I walk through the valley of the shadow of death ...

# SCENE SEVEN

*BILLY and RUSSELL are back in the police station with*
*OFFICER DELAIRE.*

OFFICER DELAIRE

So just to get this straight, all of this, $17,000 in damages,
over thirty charges of disturbing the peace, damaging public
property, assault, and a dozen other miscellaneous charges, are
all because of an ex-girlfriend? That's a bit much to believe.

BILLY

Oh come on, Officer, everybody has one person in their
past, an ex-something that ... no matter how much time
passes, or how many miles are between you, the history or
misunderstanding between the two of you just grows and
festers, till something sets it off. Some chance encounter, or act
of God, or an indigenous land dispute.

RUSSELL

We've all got one. Mine is in the band. I'm sure even for you,
somewhere in your recent or more distant history, there was a
somebody you once cared about who holds a special place in
your heart no matter how many years pass. If you were to run
into them today, because of your shared history, things might
not turn out so well.

*OFFICER DELAIRE looks down at his desk blotter, lost in*
*thoughts of the past. Suddenly he snaps out of it.*

OFFICER DELAIRE

That's ... that's not ... we're deviating from the point here. Let's
get back to you. So you're just innocent victims in all this?

RUSSELL

Totally. Just luck of the draw.

BILLY

Random chance. We're just innocent musicians.

OFFICER DELAIRE

Okay. You were travelling to Dead Rat River. Despite all the
warnings, the danger, politically volatile situation, ex-boy band
member, you stay on the bus.

RUSSELL

By the time all this sunk in, we were committed.

BILLY

And we didn't want to piss off Buck by asking him to turn
around. He seemed kind of volatile.

OFFICER DELAIRE

And this Sadie Thompson. Where does she fit into all this,
above and beyond being your ex-girlfriend?

BILLY

It's complicated.

OFFICER DELAIRE

Simplify it.

BILLY

Well …

OFFICER DELAIRE

Well?

BILLY

Well … turns out, it turns out … she turns out … How to put
this … She was my cousin.

OFFICER DELAIRE

You dated your cousin?

BILLY

Yeah, but purely accidently. Honest. And when
she ... *we* ... found out, well she took it kind of badly. Women
can be like that, you know. So you put all these different
elements into this mixing pot called Dead Rat River and, well,
this is where things started to get weird. Right, Russell?

RUSSELL

Testify.

# END OF ACT ONE

# ACT TWO

# SCENE ONE

*Still in the police station. On the desk between OFFICER DELAIRE and the two men is an open pizza box. All three are enjoying a slice and some pop.*

OFFICER DELAIRE

So you're travelling five hours in a twenty-year-old school bus to end up in a potentially volatile situation. There's a woman at the other end of this journey who has expressed extreme hostile intentions for one of you should you set foot in Dead Rat River. You're not making any money to perform. And everybody else has pulled out of this concert event due to hazard risks. Have I got this right?

RUSSELL

We really need to hire a legitimate booking agent.

OFFICER DELAIRE

I'm not superstitious or anything like that, but what more do you need to know before it occurs to you this might not be a good idea? A burning bush? A decapitated cow?

BILLY

Sure, this is all 20/20 hindsight. Everything is obvious that way.

OFFICER DELAIRE

So what exactly did you know about the DRR conflict?

RUSSELL

Just what Billy and Buck told us.

BILLY

It's just the usual story. Native people own the land but not the resources underneath. Some copper ore is discovered and now everybody wants a slice of the pie. Federal, provincial, municipal, and corporate people try to bully the Native people. Then they discover Native people don't want to be bullied around. Same old, same old.

RUSSELL

Yeah, that.

BILLY

The dispute intensifies ...

OFFICER DELAIRE

Barricades go up.

RUSSELL

I thought it was to keep the crowds back. You know, from rushing the stage.

BILLY

He actually did believe that.

OFFICER DELAIRE

And this Sadie Thomas woman ...

BILLY

Thompson. Sadie Thompson.

OFFICER DELAIRE

Right, Thompson. It says here ...

BILLY

I'm sure whatever she said, she exaggerated.

OFFICER DELAIRE

Okay. Tell me about her. Other than the fact she's your cousin. Your ... kissing cousin.

BILLY

She ... she has issues.

OFFICER DELAIRE

We all have issues. I have issues. My dog has issues. Issues in general ... Or issues just specifically with you?

BILLY

Well, it depends on how you interpret reality.

OFFICER DELAIRE

It usually does.


## SCENE TWO

*Everybody is still on the bus. BUCK is talking.*

BUCK

Yeah, seriously. In my younger years, I also used to drive stock cars too. That's why I love highway driving.

*He shifts gears and floors it. Everybody leans dangerously to the left as BUCK makes a radical lane change.*

JENNIFER

Our Father who art in Heaven ...

*RUSSELL comes from the back of the bus, carrying some drinks for everybody. He passes them out.*

RUSSELL

Hey take it easy there, Buck.

BUCK

Just because your people invented the internal combustion engine, doesn't give you the right to tell me how to drive. Quit oppressing me.

*BUCK makes another radical lane change.*

JOANNE

Don't ... Don't ... don't aggravate him. Any idea what we're gonna do when we get there?

RUSSELL

Hey. I didn't book this. I'm not the leader, remember? Just a nameless member of this democratic collective. Why aren't you asking Billy?

ANDY

(*rhyming*)

*It seems our friend Billy doesn't feel like talking.*
*Turns out Buck's news was a little too shocking.*

RUSSELL

Billy! Snap out of it. Maybe you'd care to fill us in on the tale of Sadie Thompson and what we're getting into.

PAULINE

Might as well. We've got time to kill.

*BILLY has been lying down on a free seat near the back. Brooding. Reluctantly, he rejoins them.*

BILLY

Well ... you'll laugh at this ... really ...

RUSSELL

Oh great. I need a good laugh. Make me laugh, Billy. Please make me laugh.

BILLY

We dated for about a year and a half.

RUSSELL

Your cousin?! You never, like, noticed her at any of the family functions? Sitting across from you at Christmas dinner? Passing in the hallway at school? Going trick-or-treating together? Or is this some sort of "Native thing"?

BILLY

No, you're misunderstanding the whole thing.

RUSSELL

I hope so.

JOANNE

How can you not know you're dating your cousin? What little I know about Native communities is that practically everybody knows everybody else's business. This is a hard thing not to notice.

JENNIFER

There are entire passages in the Bible about this kind of stuff.

PAULINE

Everybody, let Billy explain.

RUSSELL

And you're okay with this?

PAULINE

As I said, let him explain. Billy?

BILLY

What you don't know is my uncle used to play for the Otter
Lake Warriors, a baseball team. My mother's older brother.
The team was quite good. They played all over the province,
tournaments and stuff, including where Sadie's from. He ran
into her mom. Spent a couple weeks together and so on. The
rest of that part of the story I think you can figure out. Flash
forward twenty years. Sadie and I bump into each other at
her community's powwow. We hit it off. Started hanging out
together in Toronto. Again, you can figure out the rest of that
by yourself.

JOANNE

So how ... how did you find out about each other?

RUSSELL

This should be good.

BILLY

Well, I finally took her home to meet the family. My uncle
was there for a barbecue, and the usual questions popped up,
like, Where are you from? Who do you know? Who are your
parents? What year were you born? The usual stuff. Didn't take
long for my uncle to put two and two together ...

JENNIFER

What happened?

BILLY

I guess you could say Sadie didn't take it well. Fastest breakup
I've ever had. I mean, I told her, Look at the bigger picture.
We didn't know. It wasn't our fault. It just happened.

JOANNE

I can't get this image out of my mind now, all my cousins
sitting in a hot tub with me. Naked. ( *she shivers* ) And now she
hates you.

JENNIFER

Wow, I have four cousins, and I couldn't ever imagine dating any of them. Of course they're all under fourteen ... and girls ... but still ...

RUSSELL

There's dislike, and then there's murderous rage. Why does this Sadie Thompson seem to be leaning towards that end of the spectrum? I mean, this is embarrassing but ...

PAULINE

I agree. It's completely out of proportion. Who here hasn't made a silly and embarrassing mistake like this?

ANDY/JENNIFER/JOANNE/BUCK

Like this? Not me. Are you kidding? There are laws against this. No way, Jose.

BILLY

That was about three years ago or so. I read somewhere that tragedy plus time equals comedy. Who ever said that has never met Sadie.

JENNIFER

Wow. And she's from this Dead Rat River?

BILLY

She's not from DRR, but evidently she's living there now. Lucky us.

BUCK

With the chief.

BILLY

With the chief. Heading their version of the local Warrior Society.

PAULINE

The point is, this is not Billy's fault. Well, it is kinda both of theirs but not to the point of her threatening to kill him. It just happened and Billy has moved on. But she hasn't. I say we just ignore it and move on. Technically, it's not really an issue anymore. Just to her.

ANDY

(rhyming)

*Yet another sad tale of tragic love between a he and she.*
*Still, are we gonna pull over soon? I really have to pee.*

JENNIFER

I was not expecting all this. She sounds dangerous. Should I be scared?

BILLY

I'm sure Sadie's just exaggerating. Nothing will happen.

RUSSELL

Good, cause you're the only one she's threatening. (*to JOANNE*) I told you this was a bad idea. I told you I didn't think he was right for Cerulean Blue, but did you listen? I don't think so. Now we're going to the corner of *Apocalypse Now* and *Deliverance*.

PAULINE

Calm down, Russell.

*They all ride in silence for a few seconds.*

ANDY

(rhyming)

*I really do have to pee,*
*And that should...*

Oh fuck it. I really gotta take a whiz. Can we stop?

BUCK

Next stop isn't for twenty minutes.

ANDY

And what am I supposed to do ...

BUCK

The back door swings open. The windows open.

RUSSELL

This is rapidly becoming a nightmare.

PAULINE

If it helps, Billy is sorry. Aren't you, baby?

BILLY

Very. She's made this a very hard thing to forget. She says it gravely embarrassed her at home, with her family. Ever since then she's requested one of those ancestry.com histories from all potential dates. I think she's a little paranoid. Claims everybody knows about it and is judging her. It's all just a horrible misunderstanding.

JENNIFER

Maybe we should have had that purification ceremony.

BILLY

Probably wouldn't have helped.

JENNIFER

I thought you said I was the one who was supposed to bring guilt on this trip?

*They ride in silence for a few more seconds.*

ANDY

Hey Joanne, can you pass me that water bottle?

*She hands him a half-filled one. ANDY takes it.*

ANDY

    (*rhyming*)

*I know this seems counterproductive*
*But to a full bladder, an empty bottle is very seductive.*

    *He drains the bottle then settles low in a seat.*

JOANNE

    What are you talking ... Oh gross!

ANDY

    (*rhyming*)

*I am open to other suggestions ... Oh that feels good ...*
*In situations like this, one does what one can, not what*
    *one should.*

RUSSELL

    (*to JENNIFER*) Just another typical Cerulean Blue tour.

## SCENE THREE

    *Later that afternoon. The bus arrives and finally stops in Dead Rat*
    *River First Nations, a secluded field with some teepees scattered*
    *around. The door opens. Two Native women, RUBY and LENORE,*
    *stand by, waiting.*

BUCK

    Welcome to wonderful downtown Dead Rat River. Please
    mind your footing as you exit the bus. And remember, if you
    hear popping or ricocheting sounds, please duck.

    *One by one, stiff and tired Cerulean Blue members exit the bus.*
    *They stretch and look around.*

JENNIFER

    I am not sure I understand the Native sense of humour.

BUCK

I am going to park the bus over there by the fence, where you can unload all your equipment when you want. Thank you for flying Air Buck.

*BUCK and the bus exit.*

ANDY

(*rhyming*)

*Everyone, this is why I absolutely hate to tour.*
*Another reason why I refuse to go north of Bloor.*

LENORE

(*consults clipboard*) Excuse me, are you people the ... Norwegian Stew?

RUSSELL

Oh for Christ's sake ...

JENNIFER

Excuse me. I would appreciate your not taking the Lord's name in vain.

RUSSELL

Why not? They're taking ours in vain. It's Cerulean Blue. Cerulean Blue. Say it with me: "Cerulean Blue."

LENORE

Cerulean Blue. And just what is a Cerulean Blue? I mean, I know what a Norwegian Stew is, but I've never heard of a Cerulean Blue.

RUSSELL

It's a colour, a shade of blue. Kind of a cobalt, azure shade. Sort of a metaphor for the kind of modernist blues music we encapsulate ...

LENORE

Cobalt ... Azure ... So technically, your group name is ... Blue
blue? I like Norwegian Stew better. Whatever, welcome to
Dead Rat River First Nation. My name is Lenore and this
here is Ruby.

*RUBY waves.*

LENORE

We're the organizers of the Dead Rat River National Save Our
Traditional Lands and Rights Music Festival, which, I assume
you have been informed, has been downgraded to ( *checks
clipboard again* ) An Evening with Norwegian Stew, which
obviously we will have to change.

JOANNE

We just went through some sort of checkpoint. There were lots
of people with lots of weapons. It looked kind of scary.

LENORE

Yes, it has made going to the Tim Hortons kind of difficult.
Oh well, war is hell. Now this is where you will be staying ...

RUSSELL

Where will we be staying?

LENORE

Here.

RUSSELL

What "here"? This is a field.

LENORE

Nothing gets by you city boys, does it? Yes, this is a field.
And on this field, over there, you will find some teepees. That
is your accommodation till An Evening with Norwegian
Stew is over.

JENNIFER

My goodness, teepees ... Who would have thought we'd be
staying in teepees?!

RUSSELL

This is a Native reserve.

PAULINE

Actually teepees are more indigenous to the prairies. Over
the years, much like totem poles, they have become quite
ubiquitous as symbols of Native culture. Almost to the
point where practically every Native community will have
representations of Native cultures from all parts of the country
scattered through their village, be they inukshuks or dream
catchers. I believe, traditionally, this was wigwam territory.

LENORE

Let me guess, your Indian name is She-Who-Reads-Too-Many-
National-Geographics. Yes, these are teepees. Now normally
we would put you up at the Holiday Inn but at the moment,
they don't seem interested in taking any reservations from
the reserve. So as usual, we have to adapt. Movement and
accommodations are a little stressed at the moment – you can
thank your government for that – and we were lucky enough to
get you these teepees, left over from a tourist event we held last
month. Look, two are even blue blue.

JENNIFER

How rustic. And what about the washrooms?

LENORE

That's even more rustic. The porta-potty will be delivered in
the morning.

ANDY

(*rhyming*)

*Shitting with the raccoons and peeing with the deer,*
*Tell me someone, how far away is the Annex from here?*

LENORE

You know, we have a wilderness camping program on the reserve that caters to taking middle-class white people out in the bush to be one with the land and frolic in the bulrushes like our ancestors did. We usually charge a thousand a pop for that. So consider this a freebie, a fringe benefit. I believe the proper term for you entertainment people is "swag."

RUSSELL

Crap ...

LENORE

If you must, in that ditch over there till the porta-potty arrives.

*RUBY spots BILLY and nudges LENORE.*

LENORE

Hey, you're Billy Burroughs, aren't you?

BILLY

Me? Yeah. Why?

LENORE

No reason. No reason at all. Your reputation precedes you.

*RUBY and LENORE stare at him for a moment, peering into his soul.*

LENORE

Very interesting. Oh well, any other questions?

PAULINE

Your friend there doesn't say much.

LENORE

Ruby's on a language fast.

PAULINE

Do I have to ask?

LENORE

For the next week, she will not speak any English. Only
Anishinabe, what you may know as Ojibway. That is a language
fast. It's a journey Ruby has decided to take, to improve her
willpower and help generate self-discipline, while paying
respect to her heritage. It's a Native thing.

*RUBY gives them a thumbs-up.*

LENORE

Now, will there be anything else?

JOANNE

We are really starved. Somebody mentioned something about
some fresh fish for dinner.

LENORE

Each teepee is equipped with a frying pan and a fishing
rod. The lake is half a mile in that direction. Go nuts. All
our hospitality staff are busy at the barricades, so the entire
community is operating at a bare minimum. We are happy to
have you here. We appreciate any help we can get. Right, Ruby?

*Once again, RUBY gives an enthusiastic thumbs-up.*

LENORE

Okay then. I suggest you all get a good night's sleep. I'll be back
in the morning to fill you in on tomorrow night's concert.

JENNIFER

Excuse me but are there any wolves or coyotes or things like that around here that we should be worried about?

LENORE

Nope. The bears scared them away. Ain't that right, Ruby?

*RUBY briefly acts and sounds like a scary bear, then a scared coyote or wolf running away.*

JENNIFER

Oh my goodness!

LENORE

Sleep tight. See you tomorrow.

JOANNE

You're not staying?

LENORE

Nope, running late already. I have to sneak through the barricades and drive an hour south to Baymeadow. I'm in a community production of this play, a musical. Ever heard of *Les Misérables*?

RUSSELL

You're kidding?!

LENORE

You don't think Native people can be eclectic? (*singing*) "I dreamed a dream ..." Sure, hire the Native woman to play the prostitute. Typical. After the show's done, I may have to file a human-rights complaint.

*RUBY gives her another thumbs-up.*

RUSSELL

How ironic ...

LENORE

How is that ironic?

RUSSELL

You're in a musical about rebellion and barricades. And you're
here, involved in both.

LENORE

Yes, I can see the irony practically dripping from the barrels of
all those guns. And I don't think *Les Miz* is a good role model
for what may happen here. We're a little more optimistic. Oh,
by the way, you guys do any AC/DC?

RUSSELL

No.

LENORE

I thought one of the first rules of show business is know your
audience.

*The two women exit the campground.*

JOANNE

Russell, if it's possible, the shit we are in has just gotten a foot
deeper. And us without a ladder.

ANDY

(*rhyming*)

*Russell, pulling things out of the water is never my wish*
*Even as a kid, I never played that stupid game, Go Fish.*

Let me go home. I'll drum by Skype.

RUSSELL

Why are you all coming to me? This isn't my mess.
Mr. Burroughs is the gentleman you should be appealing to.

PAULINE

Russell, leave Billy alone. He never meant for any of this
to happen.

BILLY

No he's right, Pauline. This is all my fault. With Sadie, with
joining the band, with bringing us up here to this mess. Not
one thing has gone right.

*Everybody is silent.*

JOANNE

This is not a matter of assigning blame. We all agreed to
come up here ...

RUSSELL

I said not to.

PAULINE

Yes, Russell, we know. No wonder Mom and Dad wanted to
send you to military school in Kingston.

RUSSELL

Hey, I'm not the one who disappeared to a kibbutz in Israel for
a year. And we're not even Jewish.

PAULINE

I was trying to find myself.

RUSSELL

News flash! I found you, and guess where I found you? Behind
the barricades at a place called Dead Rat River First Nation.

You've been on a hell of a long journey just to end up here. You
keep looking in everybody else's backyard except your own.

PAULINE

At least I'm out there looking, not trying to make the world
do what I want, or even put it in order. I have done things you
would never believe. I have seen places that defy description.
I have met people who've changed my life and whose lives I've
changed. That's a little more important than running a band
nobody wants you to run.

   *Beat.*

JOANNE

Well, past experience has taught me that between these two,
this could take forever. I'm going to bed. This sibling squabble
was old two years ago. I got this teepee. Jennifer, you take the
blue one over there. Andy, take the yellow one way across the
field. Way across the field. You guys figure out your own. Good
night, you two, I'm going to get my stuff out of the bus, then set
up my grassroots accommodation. ( *to PAULINE and RUSSELL* )
You two try not to get any blood on the teepees.

BILLY

But it's early, the sun is still up.

JOANNE

Yeah but that bus trip just about killed me. And they could be
at this for hours. One Thanksgiving when I was with Russell,
I put a turkey in just as they got started, when they finished I
had to throw it out. Besides, I'm beat.

JENNIFER

To tell you the truth, so am I. Wow, take a look at all those big
trees and all that magnificent and mysterious forest. It's just like
something out of *A Midsummer Night's Dream*.

JOANNE

Then let's get the puck out of here.

*JENNIFER walks towards her teepee. ANDY follows her until JOANNE realizes what he's doing.*

JOANNE

(*shouting*) ANDY!!!

*ANDY changes course to his own teepee. They all exit the stage, leaving behind the remaining three, still breathing with emotion.*

RUSSELL

Pauline?

PAULINE

Russell?

RUSSELL

Even though this has been said before, by many others to many other others, I say this as honestly as one brother can possibly say to his sister. Bite me.

PAULINE

Sorry but one side effect of living on that kibbutz for a year is I don't eat pork.

*Pissed off, RUSSELL walks to his teepee.*

BILLY

You two have some issues.

PAULINE

He only sees himself at the centre of the world, he doesn't see the world around him. I guess that teepee is ours. Hmm, looks Plains Cree, possibly Assiniboine. You coming?

BILLY

Not yet. I'm not tired. I'm a little wound up. I'm going to hang out here for a while.

PAULINE

Billy, don't let all this get you down. I'm sure everything will be okay. I have faith in you. I have faith in how things will turn out.

BILLY

I just hope I don't let you down.

PAULINE

There's no way you could do that. This fear you have of performing ... It's just a little speed bump on the road of life. It's an irrational fear, and they may be the most stubborn, but they are also the weakest. I'll get our stuff.

*PAULINE exits, leaving behind a despondent BILLY. He surveys the land around him, sighs, and gathers up some sticks. He is putting together a fire.*

BILLY

( *singing to himself* ) "There's no business like show business ... no business I know ..."

## SCENE FOUR

*Later. The sun has set, and BILLY is tending a fire alone. After a few seconds, RUSSELL emerges from his teepee, yawning and stretching. He sees BILLY and debates whether or not to go over, but having limited options, he saunters over to the fire.*

RUSSELL

Hey.

BILLY

Have a good nap?

RUSSELL

It's been a long time since I slept on the ground. People pay a thousand dollars for this?

BILLY

Thirteen hundred if you want a lean-to built by an actual real-life Aboriginal, according to Buck. There's a course on lean-to building at the college.

RUSSELL

Really?! Wow.

BILLY

White people can be stupid.

*They both share a laugh.*

BILLY

Russell, you'll be happy to know ... I'm thinking of leaving.

RUSSELL

Leaving?! Leaving what?!

BILLY

The band. Here. Everything that's wrong now started with me. Maybe it's better if I leave. Safer anyways.

RUSSELL

Look, sorry if I came down hard on you earlier. I was a little angry and tensions were running a little thick. You leaving won't solve the problems. If anything, it will make things worse.

BILLY

That's nice of you to say but let's face reality here …

RUSSELL

What about Pauline?

BILLY

I got the impression you two weren't really that close.

RUSSELL

Let's pretend I am.

BILLY

You see, I don't know …

RUSSELL

You don't know. You're making all these big decisions and you don't know. Don't you think you should before you decide a course of action?

BILLY

I thought you didn't like me.

RUSSELL

I'm just thinking about the band. And my sister. Besides, where are you gonna go? You're deep in hostile territory and I don't think the cavalry comes to the rescue anymore.

*BILLY gives him a peculiar look.*

RUSSELL

Bad choice of metaphors I know.

BILLY

I think there's something else I should tell you.

RUSSELL

Oh God, what now?

BILLY

I wasn't really that interested in joining your band. Playing
in front of people. I really wasn't. It was your sister who
pushed me.

RUSSELL

I knew you were one of her make-work projects. Why? You in
some sort of witness-relocation project?

BILLY

No. But I have a ... I guess you could call it a crippling fear of
performing in public. More than a dozen people watching me
and I curl up into a fetal position. Both literally and figuratively.

RUSSELL

I see the problem.

BILLY

Grade eight school concert. I was onstage. Playing my guitar.
A string broke. My voice broke. I peed myself. All in that order.
That was the last time I was onstage. I'm sorry, man, I think this
is a case of false representation. Your sister, she doesn't seem to
understand that there are some things that really scare people.
More people fear performing in public than dying. Everything's
a challenge to her. I really admire that. And I really hate that.

RUSSELL

You should have told us. I mean, not just me. This matters to
the whole band.

BILLY

I know. But she told me not to. She thinks, when push comes
to shove, everything will be ... okay.

RUSSELL

I wonder what colour the sky is in her world.

*They both laugh.*

BILLY

That's one of the reasons I think I should leave.

RUSSELL

Why are you so scared?! I mean, we all get a little nervous every time we perform. It's a good thing. Gets the adrenaline flowing.

BILLY

I don't know. It makes me uncomfortable when people look at me. Maybe cause I come from a big family. Everybody was so loud and outgoing. And usually every time I was the centre of attention, it was not a good thing. I used to get teased and picked on a lot. Or blamed. It was always better to fly under the radar.

RUSSELL

Hmm, and what were you going to do tomorrow night? Onstage, when we started into our first song?

BILLY

Well, either play along. Or pee myself. I don't see much middle ground.

RUSSELL

You do know most of our equipment is electrical?

BILLY

I envy guys like you. I can tell you love it up there.

RUSSELL

> More than love it. I need it. More accurately, the band needs it.
> What we're all waiting for is that "snap," you know, that comes
> when everything is just right. When I'm up there, and Joanne
> and the rest are just solid, and we're a band and we're hot,
> we feel a snap. Call it a runner's high or a rush of endorphins,
> whatever you want to call it. But that's why we do what we
> do. We sure don't do it for the money or the fame. That's a
> laugh. We do it to feel that snap. Once we got that, makes all
> this worth it.

BILLY

> A snap, huh? Maybe I should try that.

> *Suddenly they hear a noise off to the side. Four people
> approach: SADIE, RUBY, OTTER, and ARTHUR.*

RUSSELL

> Seems we got some guests. Fans, do you think?

BILLY

> Oh shit. Just the opposite. I do believe that's Sadie and I think
> that's that Ruby woman, and I don't know the other two.

RUSSELL

> That's the famous Sadie?! She seems so tiny.

BILLY

> So's a bullet.

> *The new quartet stop just short of the fire. They size each
> other up.*

SADIE

> Billy Burroughs. Either you didn't get my message or you
> ignored it.

BILLY

Hi, Sadie. You're looking good.

SADIE

Are you trying to make small talk with me? Are you
that stupid?

BILLY

I missed you too. Who are your friends?

SADIE

This is Arthur, my boyfriend and chief of Dead Rat River.

ARTHUR

On behalf of Dead Rat River First Nations, I'd like to thank you
for taking time out of your busy schedule and donating your
talents to helping us in this difficult time of struggle. (*beat*)
As Sadie's boyfriend, I'm going to beat your fucking head in.

SADIE

And I think you know Ruby.

*RUBY gives him the finger.*

SADIE

And this is Otter, Ruby's interpreter while she's on the
language fast.

*RUBY gives them another finger, then elbows OTTER.*

OTTER

Ah ... "Fuck off."

BILLY

This is Russell Aymes. He's the ...

SADIE

I don't care who he is. I sent a message letting you know
you aren't wanted here. Just because you're in some two-bit
blues band ...

RUSSELL

Hey, hate the guy but don't hate the band.

SADIE

... hasn't changed anything. Married your sister yet?

BILLY

They're all married ... but that's not the point. Jesus, Sadie, that
was a long time ago and it wasn't my fault. It wasn't anybody's
fault. It was just one of those things that happened.

SADIE

One of these things ... Your family sends me invites to all the
family gatherings. Your uncle – my so-called father – keeps
wanting to know what I want for my birthday and Christmas.
My so-called half-sister is in some sort of financial difficulty
and the collection agency has started calling me. Somebody
put me on the emailing list for a porn site called Keep It in the
Family. Your aunt needs a kidney and wants to know if I'm
using both of mine ... do you get where I'm going with this ...

BILLY

That's the funny thing. The reserve has such defined
boundaries yet my family doesn't.

SADIE

And I think you always knew.

BILLY

No, you're being ridiculous. There's no way I knew.

SADIE

You commented how we dressed the same.

BILLY

That doesn't mean anything. We dressed in black. Everybody
dresses in black. And you should see this guy and his sister.
They don't dress anything alike.

SADIE

We like the same things. We have the same hair and eyes.

BILLY

We have the same hair and eyes because we're both Native.

RUSSELL

Have you guys thought of ... I don't know ... seeing a therapist
or mediator?! I hear they can do wonders.

*RUBY mimes a message.*

OTTER

Ruby says ... "Shut up, you asshole."

RUSSELL

I liked it better when you were on your language fast.

*RUBY mimes again.*

OTTER

That ... was I think something about your mother and a
hockey team ...

*Sound of a rustling behind them and PAULINE crawls out of the
teepee, awakened by the discussion.*

BILLY

Oh great ...

RUSSELL

Ah Pauline, maybe you should ...

PAULINE

What's going on? Who are your friends?

*RUBY nudges SADIE and points.*

OTTER

That's the one, she says.

SADIE

Your new squeeze.

BILLY

How did you know?

SADIE

Why do you think I sent Sadie in? Information. Nice to know you're dating outside the family. ( *looking at PAULINE* ) She's cute. Just like your wine preference – something cold and white, rather than warm and red.

RUSSELL

Hey, that's my sister you're ...

ARTHUR

As chief, I must urge you to remain neutral in this situation. It is an internal issue best left to those personally involved in this particular conflict. ( *beat* )As Sadie's boyfriend, interrupt her again and I will beat your fucking head in.

SADIE

Just leave, Billy. You're not wanted here. Don't play tomorrow night or things could get ugly. This is my territory now. You're alone here. Just a friendly word of warning.

BILLY

How friendly?

SADIE

All things considered, not that friendly.

PAULINE

(*approaching*) Did I miss something?

SADIE

No, we were just leaving. Bye.

*SADIE and RUBY turn to leave.*

ARTHUR

As chief, I can't tell you how grateful Dead Rat River First
Nation is to have you perform tomorrow night on their benefit.
Your participation in this event has already strengthened our
position and supported our fight. (*beat*) As Sadie's boyfriend,
show up tomorrow night and I'll beat your fucking head in.

RUSSELL

You know, I had one ex-girlfriend cut up all my clothes. All
things considered, I think I got off easy. I could actually feel the
hate coming off her in waves.

PAULINE

What was all that about?

BILLY

That was Sadie.

PAULINE

Her? Wow, she looks so small.

RUSSELL

So does a bullet I'm told. Now admittedly, I don't know many
Native customs but that sounded like a threat to me. A threat
that says we shouldn't perform tomorrow. What should we do?

PAULINE

She threatened you?! If she didn't want us here, and her
boyfriend is chief, why did Cerulean Blue get an official invite
in the first place?

BILLY

He may be chief, but the Dead Rat River Defence League
includes the council and several members of the community.
He was probably outvoted.

RUSSELL

So what are we going to do?

PAULINE

Billy honey, I was thinking. Maybe we should all leave. Get the
hell out of here. I hate backing down in the face of a blatant
abuse of power but this whole thing has a bad feel to it. This
probably isn't the best place for your debut with Cerulean Blue.
Especially with your ... um ... problem ...

RUSSELL

I know about his problem. Nice of you to let me know.

PAULINE

Let's just say I knew you wouldn't be very supportive. Now,
about leaving ...

BILLY

Do you know how to drive a bus?

PAULINE

We'll get a cab.

RUSSELL

A five-hour cab ride. *We'd* have to pawn all our equipment.

BILLY

No. Russell was right.

PAULINE

He was?!

RUSSELL

That's good to know. What was I right about?

BILLY

The only point in running is having a place to run to. You're
here. The band is here. Where am I going to run to?

RUSSELL

Just five minutes ago …

BILLY

… was five minutes ago. A lot can happen in five minutes.
According all those physicists and their Big Bang theory,
everything in the universe was created in something like
half a second.

*A voice calls out from JENNIFER's teepee.*

JENNIFER

( *offstage* ) Everything was created in six days.

PAULINE

Are you sure this is a good idea?

BILLY

No, but it's the only one I have.

*JOANNE emerges from the bushes.*

JOANNE

I thought I heard voices. Anybody catch any fish yet?

RUSSELL

Where were you?

JOANNE

Visiting the ditch. Charming place, really. A family of raccoons watched me.

*Suddenly, a pair of headlights bathe them in bright light.*

RUSSELL

Oh God, it's not them again, is it?

JOANNE

Who again?

BILLY

(*pointing in the opposite direction*)
They left that way. I don't know who ...

*The lights go out and ASHLEY comes running up to them.*

ASHLEY

Here you are! I've been looking all over for you guys. It took me forever to find out where you were.

JOANNE

Ashley? What the hell are you doing here? Where's Casey?

ASHLEY

Casey is a bastard. A really horrible bastard. I left him.

RUSSELL

It's only been a week.

ASHLEY

A lot can happen in a week. It's over. We're through. I couldn't stay in the same city with him. I needed some time away. I needed my friends. So I thought I'd, like ... come up and join you guys.

PAULINE

You drove all the way up here?

BILLY

That must have been some fight.

RUSSELL

Ashley, you don't drive. How did you get here?

*HELENA, Ashley's mother, saunters in, looking greatly displeased.*

HELENA

I smoke one cigarette during my pregnancy and this is the daughter I get. Where are we? *The Gulag Archipelago?*

PAULINE

How did you get across the barricades? They said they were closing off the roads.

HELENA

Darling, I was raised in Lebanon. Canadians don't know the first thing about decent barricades. Now, if somebody can point me to the nearest Four Seasons ...

RUSSELL

Ashley, you know we hired a new keyboardist. You were out of the band.

ASHLEY

You are going to let me back in, aren't you? I need you, the band ...

JOANNE

What happened to the whole it's-a-new-world thing you wanted to grab hold of?

ASHLEY

I may have exaggerated. You see, I realized there was nothing wrong with the old world.

HELENA

Oh, just let her do her piano thing. It'll make her happy. Where is that young man who talks funny? He amuses me.

RUSSELL

The problem is, what would we do with Jennifer?

*JENNIFER emerges from her teepee.*

JENNIFER

I heard my name. What's going on out here? Are we having a party?

ASHLEY

Is that her?

HELENA

Why are we standing in the middle of a field?

JOANNE

It's a long story.

BILLY

I don't know any of these people. I think I'll go to bed.

PAULINE

Maybe I'll join you. (*to JOANNE*) You can fill us in later.

*They exit into a teepee.*

ASHLEY

Do you know how hard it is to find Dead Rat River? Most of the people we asked thought we'd made the name up.

HELENA

They said they were going to bed. Why are they going into those triangle things?

JENNIFER

Russell, introduce me.

RUSSELL

Okay, Jennifer, this is Ashley and this is Helena, her mother.

JENNIFER

I am so delighted to meet you. Welcome. We've had quite the adventure.

HELENA

I don't do adventure. (*still looking at the teepees*) That movie ... *Dances with* ... something ... That's where I've seen those things. Ashley honey, we're here now. I'm tired. I need less field and more martini. Do something.

ASHLEY

Yes, Mother. (*to JENNIFER*) Hello.

*There is an awkward silence. ANDY crawls out of his teepee, stretches, and notices all the new people.*

ANDY

(*rhyming*)

*Man, I'm hungry. I'd kill for some chicken wings.*
*Ashley? Helena? What time is it? Did I miss something?*

ASHLEY

Andy, I'm divorcing Casey.

ANDY

(*rhyming*)

*See what happens when we leave the city. Divorces, threats,*
*nothing to be eaten,*
*Let's go home where there's love, peace, and definitely lots and*
*lots of chicken.*

HELENA

(*to ANDY*) Hello, darling.

ANDY

(*rhyming*)

*Oh my, my,*
*Mama's apple pie.*


# SCENE FIVE

*The Dead Rat River Community Hall. Midday. The band set up*
*their equipment. Other people mill about setting up chairs and*
*other concert equipment. BILLY and RUSSELL work with the*
*amplifiers.*

BILLY

This is the last chance to change our minds. Better and smarter
bands than us would be kicking stones to the next town. Not
every band needs an Altamont.

RUSSELL

Cerulean Blue doesn't run.

BILLY

Has Cerulean Blue ever been in a situation like this before?

RUSSELL

No, but it's the principle. We're a blues band. We're supposed
to be used to trouble. The more trouble, the better the blues.

BILLY

I guess. But you don't strike me as the troubled sort.

RUSSELL

Try spending two years with Joanne. Try kicking some
lyrics out of a drummer who would rather sleep or party
in Kensington Market all night. And don't get me started
on Ashley and Casey. I've lost more sleep over them than
everybody put together. And you've met my sister. I've had
my share of the blues-ish experience. It doesn't all have to
be heartbreak and depression. Sometimes it's just about the
detours in life, in trying to go from A to B. ( *pause* ) Speaking of
which, how're you doing? I mean, nervous-wise?

BILLY

Fighting every possible impulse to run out that door and keep
running. I keep looking at the clock. Fingers are cold.

RUSSELL

Not good in a guitarist.

BILLY

Sure you still want me onstage?

RUSSELL

It's all the same. If you quit now, no guitarist for the show.
If you go onstage and then find yourself unable to play, still no
guitarist. But on the off chance my sister is right and you do
pull it together, we have a guitarist. A small chance is better
than no chance. Sometimes plugging the hole of an inside
straight with the river card can actually happen.

BILLY

Wow, that's almost deep. Thanks for the support … I think.

RUSSELL

Of course, that's assuming nothing else out of hand happens tonight. You do lead an interesting life, Mr. Burroughs.

BILLY

What's that old saying … May you live in interesting times. Whoever said that, I don't think they've ever dated their cousin. (*pause*) Hey Russell, ever been in a fight?

RUSSELL

Sure I have. Joanne's tougher than she looks. She has this way of kicking your knee out from directly beneath you. Took two semesters of physical training when she was going to university to be a cop. Way back when.

BILLY

Joanne? Really?

RUSSELL

Oh yeah. Only dropped out when touring with the band screwed up her grades. The late nights and later mornings. That's kind of when we broke up. Kind of blamed me for it.

BILLY

But she's still with the band?

RUSSELL

What can I say? She loves the music.

BILLY

Or maybe still you?

RUSSELL

Oh no. That ship has sailed. Long ago. Long, long, long ago. I'm
barely tolerated. Some things in this world should not happen.
Metallica doing an Elton John tribute album is probably one of
them. Planting a vineyard in Nunavut is another. And Joanne
and me trying to hammer out a relationship is definitely on
that list. We're lucky there were no civilian casualties involved
when things ended. And we weren't related.

BILLY

Very funny. Well, you got me to fight with now.

RUSSELL

Don't forget Pauline. Actually, your annoyance factor has
been greatly reduced. I don't know if I would be as calm in a
situation like this if I were you. I'm not good with surprises.
I like a cool, planned, well-orchestrated tour.

*They work a bit longer. JENNIFER wanders over.*

JENNIFER

Hey Billy, what's that building next door? I keep seeing a lot of
babies going in and out.

BILLY

I was told that's the prenatal clinic. If Dead Rat River is
anything like Otter Lake, most of the babies on this reserve
were probably conceived in the community hall parking lot
after the dances. So I guess it made sense to put the prenatal
clinic right beside it. One-stop shopping. It's a ...

RUSSELL

... Native thing?

JENNIFER

I'm going to go look at some of the babies.

RUSSELL

Excuse me, have you finished setting up your keyboards?!

JENNIFER

No, but I'm almost …

RUSSELL

"Almost" is not finished. No baby-watching till your work is done, young lady.

*A disappointed JENNIFER turns and leaves.*

JENNIFER

Ahh …

RUSSELL

It's like being a father. ( *pause* ) Think they'll be any trouble tonight?

BILLY

I'm thinking positive. There will positively not be any trouble tonight.

RUSSELL

I've tried that positive-thinking thing. It doesn't work a lot of the time. You still got that sweet grass handy? Just in case.

BILLY

I thought blues bands didn't purify?

RUSSELL

They don't play a lot of places called Dead Rat River either.

*JOANNE wanders over.*

JOANNE

Well, I'm set. When do you want to do the sound check?

RUSSELL

    Check with Andy. We'll need another fifteen minutes or so. I'm
    a little worried about the wiring in this place. It all looks old.
    We're going to be pulling a lot of amps out of the system.

BILLY

    You can thank the Department of Indian Affairs for its fine
    construction and maintenance of these establishments. The
    best we can do is keep our fingers and toes crossed.

RUSSELL

    You and your ancient and wise Aboriginal sayings. (*looking
    around*) Where is Andy anyway?

JOANNE

    We're not sure. If you'll notice, Helena is missing too.

RUSSELL

    (*imitating HELENA*) "The boy who talks funny. He amuses me."

JOANNE

    Exactly. You don't think…

    *JENNIFER wanders back.*

RUSSELL

    Oh my dear Lord…

JENNIFER

    That's the spirit. See, it's not so hard. Okay, I'm done.

BILLY

    (*to JOANNE*) What about your friend Ashley? Where's she?

JOANNE

> Pouting somewhere. I think she still wants to play with us but …

> *Suddenly the door swings open and CASEY is standing there, looking a little worse for wear, looking around desperately.*

CASEY

> (*shouting*) ASHLEY! ASHLEY!

RUSSELL

> This just gets stranger and stranger.

JOANNE

> Casey?! What the hell are you doing here?

CASEY

> I came to find my Ashley. I love her. I need her. I must find her. Where is she?

PAULINE

> (*overhearing*) In the toilet I think.

CASEY

> I must go to her. I will not lose her. I have crossed mountains and rivers for her … literally. (*shouting*) ASHLEY!

JOANNE

> Casey, calm down. I thought you guys had a fight?

CASEY

> It was a misunderstanding. You know, the normal Capricorn– Libra thing.

BILLY

> Oh that.

CASEY

Who are you?

JOANNE

That's Billy. He's ... uh ... the new lead guitar.

CASEY

Oh well, good luck. Have fun. I'm married and make sauces now. ( *shouting* ) ASHLEY!

*ASHLEY enters, surprised to see CASEY.*

ASHLEY

You came!

CASEY

Of course I came. There is no place you could go that I wouldn't follow you ... in a non-threatening, non-stalker, totally female-empowering manner.

ASHLEY

In a non-codependent way I was worried you wouldn't. I wasn't sure ...

CASEY

There's no place you can hide ... not even some obscure Indian reserve outside of Bumblefuck, Ontario.

BILLY

First Nations community, if you don't mind. ( *to RUSSELL* ) Does any of this make sense to you?

RUSSELL

Kinda. Their relationship has always been more dramatic. They should have been actors, not musicians.

JENNIFER

I think it's so romantic.

*ASHLEY and CASEY kiss. HELENA and ANDY enter. He has lipstick smeared all over his face and neck.*

PAULINE

Now there's something you don't see every day.

HELENA

What?! What are you looking at? Go look at something else ... oh crap. (*spotting ASHLEY and CASEY*) Here we go again. When did he show up?

JOANNE

Just now.

HELENA

She's happy. He's happy. I suppose I should be happy. (*to ANDY*) You, my little muffin, are you happy?

ANDY

(*rhyming*)

*I am always happy.*
*Happy happy happy.*

HELENA

Good for you. Wait till you hit thirty. Isn't he adorable?

JOANNE

Sure, you say that now. Wait till you have to feed and clean up after him.

BILLY

I told you white people were weird.

JENNIFER

How can you say that when your girlfriend is white?!

BILLY

Yeah but everybody looks alike in the dark.

RUSSELL

I don't need to hear that ... Okay everyone, this is all nice and fabulous. But we still have a show tonight and we're only half set up. We still have to do the sound check and do a quick rehearsal, something we are woefully short on. So if we can leave all the hugging and kissing to Casey and Ashley, maybe we can actually do something productive today. We may not have much of an audience tonight but we'll make sure they remember the group Cerulean Blue.

*This gets a rousing cheer from the band and friends. They take the stage and pick up their instruments. JENNIFER speaks quietly to ANDY. She also takes a moment to wipe some of the smeared lipstick off his face.*

JENNIFER

( *quietly* ) Hey Andy, I just heard ... that Joanne and Russell used to be an item, back when the band first got started.

ANDY

( *rhyming* )

*In the early years of Cerulean Blue, that was true
Russell and Joanne were, you could say, true blue.*

JENNIFER

Well, do you think that maybe they might get back together?! I mean, strange things have already happened on this trip, and the Good Lord does work in mysterious ways.

ANDY

(*rhyming*)

*Sweetheart, that relationship long ago met its painful and*
*timely death,*
*But it makes me wonder if you're on some Christian form of*
*crystal meth.*

RUSSELL

All right, Cerulean Blue, are we all plugged in and ready to ...

*The door opens. SADIE, ARTHUR, OTTER, RUBY, and a few others*
*walk in. They do not look pleased.*

PAULINE

Shit. Billy, it's ...

BILLY

I see them.

*A chill passes through the community hall. An uneasy BILLY*
*approaches SADIE and other members of the First Nations band,*
*who stand a few feet behind.*

SADIE

You're still here.

BILLY

Yeah. Um, I kind of hoped you were kidding. Just blowing off
some steam.

SADIE

Then you were wrong. Dead wrong.

BILLY

We aren't looking for trouble, Sadie. We're just here to perform,
like we were asked. We'll do that, then we'll leave you, this
village, and everything. Promise.

ARTHUR

> And for that, the good people of Dead Rat River First
> Nation are grateful. Support, in whatever form, is thankfully
> appreciated by its residents. ( *beat* ) Now get the hell
> out of here.

> > *RUBY gesticulates at all of them.*

OTTER

> She says you've got more people now. There weren't this many
> people getting off the bus.

SADIE

> Reinforcements?

RUSSELL

> Friends.

HELENA

> Who is this woman in the ugly shoes?

RUSSELL

> It's a long story.

HELENA

> Again with the long story. Why is everything a long story?
> I used to work in a publishing house. Synopsize!

JOANNE

> The woman with the ugly shoes is Billy's ex-girlfriend. They
> don't want us here.

HELENA

> That's your long story?!

SADIE

> There's not going to be a concert tonight.

BILLY

Sorry, but the Dead Rat River Defence League says there is.
You may be on it but I don't think you run it.

SADIE

Arthur is the chief. *We've* been checking. According to previous
band council resolutions, he does have the final say and
authority in situations like this. And he says ...

ARTHUR

... no.

*RUBY nods affirmatively.*

OTTER

"Yeah!"

ARTHUR

Considering that tensions are running quite high in the
community and surrounding area, I have decided that a
concert by Cerulean Blue would not be in the best interests
of Dead Rat River First Nation at the moment. Perhaps in the
future, when common sense has prevailed and good relations
have been restored, we can revisit the idea of hosting such a
concert. ( *beat* ) Until then, fuck off.

SADIE

You heard the man.

RUSSELL

So we're cancelled. After all this, it's been called off.

PAULINE

That's not fair.

JOANNE

Can we sue?

ANDY

> (*rhyming*)

> *We weren't getting paid, remember?*
> *We're fucked, using the vernacular.*

> *RUBY waves goodbye.*

OTTER

> Goodbye and have a nice trip.

> *RUBY disagrees with the translation.*

OTTER

> No, get lost and piss off.

> *RUBY agrees. Then there is a silence in the hall.*

BILLY

> You win.

SADIE

> There was a doubt?

JENNIFER

> What a bitch!

SADIE

> If you start packing up, you might make it out of here before
> dark. These roads can be very dangerous at night.

RUSSELL

> No.

> *RUBY responds.*

OTTER

> She says, "No? What no? What are you 'no-ing'?"

RUSSELL

We're here to perform and we're gonna perform. What's the worst that can happen?! They throw us in jail?! Hey, that's the kind of cred we need in the blues business. I say we stay – and play. Right, Billy?

BILLY

You wouldn't believe how much I want to.

SADIE

What are you talking about? He's deathly afraid of performing in public. When you showed up, I thought you were the roadie.

JOANNE

He's not. He's our lead guitarist.

SADIE

Good luck with that. But you're forgetting one thing. That's not the worse that can happen.

HELENA

Excuse me, are you threatening these young people?

ASHLEY

Uh Mom, better stay out of this.

HELENA

You, with the bad haircut. What's the worst you can do?

*RUBY seems intimidated by HELENA. She hides behind SADIE and ARTHUR.*

HELENA

That's what I thought. I have a thirteen-year-old corgi with more teeth than you.

CASEY

Helena, this may not be the place … let's go someplace and I'll buy you a martini.

ANDY

> (*rhyming*)

> *Casey's right, Helena, perhaps you should sit this one out.*
> *Until the events of this evening are no longer in doubt.*

HELENA

> Don't you worry, you sweet little man. Let Helena take care of
> this. You just sit there and look pretty.

ASHLEY

> Mom ... ?

SADIE

> In our culture we have great respect of old women but don't ...

HELENA

> Old!

> *Suddenly HELENA lashes out and punches SADIE in the face.*
> *SADIE goes sailing across the floor. RUBY catches her and they*
> *fall down. ARTHUR tries to grab HELENA but CASEY and BILLY*
> *intercede. Both sides jump into the fray. It quickly becomes a*
> *free for all. At one point RUSSELL comes to the aid of his sister.*
> *And then JOANNE to his. Anarchy has come to Dead Rat River.*


## SCENE SIX

*Back at the police station. RUSSELL, BILLY, and OFFICER*
*DELAIRE are doing the dishes from the pizza, garlic bread, and*
*salads they have ordered and eaten. OFFICER DELAIRE hands*
*them the dishes, RUSSELL washes them, and BILLY dries and*
*puts them away.*

RUSSELL

> And that's where you and the rest of your detachment come in.

OFFICER DELAIRE

> All of this because of that ex-girlfriend? Do you know how
> much damage this little altercation caused?

BILLY

> Yeah, you keep telling us. So things kind of got out of hand ...

OFFICER DELAIRE

> And that Helena woman threw the first punch? I find that
> hard to believe. From everything you told me, she seemed like
> some high-society woman who'd be afraid of breaking a nail or
> something.

RUSSELL

> Don't forget. She was raised in Lebanon. I don't know all the
> facts but supposedly there was some fighting there once. Man,
> you should have seen her go. She's small but wiry.

BILLY

> Yeah. Ninjas have nothing on those pissed-off
> Lebanese women.

OFFICER DELAIRE

> And you two guys are friends now? That seems kind of odd.

RUSSELL

> We spent seven hours in your holding cell.

BILLY

> That kind of forces you to talk.

RUSSELL

> That's where I found out he needs to be fed and watered ever
> three hours. See! I never knew that.

BILLY

That's why I was kind of crabby the first time we met. It's a blood-sugar issue that's pretty common in many Native communities.

RUSSELL

I gave him a Tootsie Pop I had in my pocket. Calmed him right down.

BILLY

And *his* compulsive need for order came from the fact he's a military brat who was moving and lived on the edge of chaos all the time. That explains Pauline too. She rebelled and went to the other end of the spectrum. Everybody should spend time in a holding cell. I think the world would probably be a much better place to live.

OFFICER DELAIRE

I'll pass that up to my superiors.

RUSSELL

And what about us?

OFFICER DELAIRE

Yes. What about you?

RUSSELL

Do we get a court date or something? Joanne's got to get back to Toronto pretty soon. She works at a Baskin Robbins. She tells me they can be quite rigid in their work-hour scheduling.

OFFICER DELAIRE

Well, you can leave when you want.

BILLY

Just like that? What about the fire? Didn't that piss them off?

OFFICER DELAIRE

Oh yes, the fire. How did that start again?

RUSSELL

I told them I didn't trust those outlets and that electrical system. You throw one Native person into a twelve-year-old amplifier and the whole circuit-breaker system goes up in smoke. ( *to BILLY* ) No offence.

BILLY

None taken. I threw two right through Andy's drum kit.

OFFICER DELAIRE

Yeah, actually, that might have been God or providence at work.

RUSSELL

Shh, don't let Jennifer hear you or we'll never hear the end of it.

OFFICER DELAIRE

No matter how pissed people are at each other, nobody wants to stand around when a prenatal clinic is in danger of burning down. It's amazing how quickly the barricades were abandoned by both sides to let the fire trucks through and then pitch in to help put out the fire. Infants in danger carry no economic or social baggage. Surprisingly, the situation has de-escalated quite a bit.

RUSSELL

Another potential disaster prevented by the blues. I think our work is done here.

OFFICER DELAIRE

Yeah. That's what I was thinking.

BILLY

So we can go?

OFFICER DELAIRE

You can go.

BILLY

( *to RUSSELL* ) We can go.

RUSSELL

Where's everybody else?

OFFICER DELAIRE

Probably waiting for you in the front lobby Mr. Burroughs, are there any other ex-girlfriends we should be aware of?! That I may need to alert the SWAT team about?

BILLY

No, the one was enough. Thank you. Bye.

RUSSELL

Thank you too, sir. I watch *Law & Order* all the time.

*BILLY and RUSSELL exit the police station.*

RUSSELL

I don't believe it! We're free! I hear all these horror stories about being arrested by the police but the worst thing I can say was the pizza was overcooked.

BILLY

Was that your first time in jail?

RUSSELL

Yeah. You?

BILLY

Yeah. You know, this might make a great song.

RUSSELL

Yeah, it might. It just might. A classic blues song. "Just spent the night in jail …"

BILLY

"I had to pee in a pail …"

RUSSELL

Maybe we should find Andy. And Joanne and the rest …

BILLY

And was I seeing things? I didn't want to say anything in front of the cop, but were you and Joanne holding hands in the paddy wagon?!

RUSSELL

Well, she did drop-kick Ruby when she was wailing away at me. Do you think Joanne still cares?

BILLY

That's what it took to play nice again? Some hundred-pound woman beating the hell out of you? Or was that some sort of Caucasian rope-a-dope?

RUSSELL

Hey, I would have won eventually. She was tiring. I'd have taken her out.

BILLY

"Taken her out"?! To what, dinner? Yet another relationship saved by a Native–non-Native brawl. I tell you, there's a ballad in there somewhere …

# SCENE SEVEN

*Cerulean Blue 3.0 gets ready to perform. The lineup consists*
*of RUSSELL, BILLY, JOANNE, CASEY, JENNIFER, ASHLEY, and*
*ANDY. The EMCEE approaches the mike.*

EMCEE

Good evening, everybody, and welcome to the Peterborough
Blues Festival. My name is Sasha and I'm your emcee for the
evening. And let me start off by saying I hope all our blues fans
are feeling in the pink tonight. Now unfortunately I'm sorry
to report, we've had a cancellation. Our opening band from
Quebec, *Les Boules bleues* has had to pull out. I can't really get
into it but, from what I'm told, it's a sensitive subject. Anyway,
we were lucky enough that the amazing band behind me was
available. I'm told they're an experimental blues band that
describes their style as an experimental and evolutionary foray
into the DNA of conventional blues music ...

JOANNE

Goddammit, Russell!

JENNIFER

I heard that.

EMCEE

Ladies and gentleman, this is Cerulean Blue 3.0.

*RUSSELL advances to the mike.*

RUSSELL

Ladies and gentlemen, speaking for the band, I can't tell you
how delighted we are to be here tonight. Both for us and for
you, because you're going to hear the first-ever concert by
the new, the improved, the renewed, the reformed Cerulean

Blue. This is a little song we concocted ourselves, about a little adventure we had up north. We hope you like it. It's called "The Dead Rat River Blues."

*RUSSELL backs up into position and looks over at BILLY.*

RUSSELL

Hey Billy, how're you doing? Okay?

BILLY

I think so. Got an extra pair of pants behind the speakers though, just in case.

RUSSELL

Then let's do it.

*The band kicks into a kick-ass version of the song.*

RUSSELL/BILLY

(*singing*)

*Now listen you all to my words of warning,*
*I have tiptoed through the streets of Heaven*
*And I've staggered across the halls of Hell.*
*I've eaten all sorts of strange and exotic foods,*
*Including something people call fennel.*

*Know that I've killed some hours by counting the bricks*
*While doing my time at the police station.*
*Nothing but nothing taught me about life*
*Like two days at Dead Rat River First Nation*

(*chorus*)

*Gotta run, gotta get out, gotta leave.*
*No place for a normal man, you gotta believe.*
*Say your prayers and pay your insurance.*
*Cuz staying sane is the best you can achieve.*

*The devil was in Georgia but stayed clear of there.*
*Dead Rat River, those people are easy to offend.*
*DDR is far away but just around the corner.*
*Especially when you're trying to avoid an ex-girlfriend.*

(*chorus*)

*Gotta run, gotta get out, gotta leave.*
*No place for a normal man, you gotta believe.*
*Say your prayers and pay your insurance.*
*Cuz staying sane is the best you can achieve.*

*Lights go down.*

— END —

# DREW HAYDEN TAYLOR

During the past twenty-five years of his life, Drew Hayden Taylor has done many things, most of which he is proud of. An Ojibway from the Curve Lake First Nations in Ontario, he has worn many hats in his literary career, from performing stand-up comedy at the Kennedy Center in Washington, D.C., to serving as artistic director of a theatre company. He is an award-winning playwright (with more than seventy productions), a journalist/columnist (appearing regularly in several Canadian newspapers and magazines), short-story writer, novelist, television scriptwriter, and has worked on more than seventeen documentaries exploring the Native experience. Most notably, he wrote and directed *Redskins, Tricksters, and Puppy Stew*, a documentary on Native humour for the National Film Board of Canada.

Hayden Taylor has travelled to seventeen countries, spreading the gospel of Native literature. Through many of his books, most notably the four-volume set of the Funny, You Don't Look Like One series, he has tried to educate and inform the world about issues that reflect, celebrate, and interfere in the lives of Canada's First Nations.

Self-described as a contemporary storyteller in whatever form, he co-created and for three years was the head writer for *Mixed Blessings*, a television comedy series, at the same time contributing scripts to four other popular Canadian television series. In 2007, a made-for-TV movie he wrote, based on his Governor General's nominated play, *In a World Created by a Drunken God* was nominated for three Gemini Awards, including Best Movie. Originally it aired on APTN and opened the American Indian Film Festival in San Francisco and the Dreamspeakers Film Festival in Edmonton.

In 2011 and 2012, he wrote the script for the National Aboriginal Achievement Awards.

The last few years has seen Hayden Taylor proudly serve as writer-in-residence at the University of Michigan, the University of Western Ontario, University of Luneburg (Germany), and Ryerson University, as well as at a host of Canadian theatre companies (Cahoots Theatre, Blyth Theatre). From 1994–97, he proudly served as the artistic director of Canada's premiere Native theatre company, Native Earth Performing Arts.

In 2007, Annick Press published his first novel, *The Night Wanderer: A Native Gothic Novel*, a teen novel about an Ojibway vampire. He has also published three non-fiction books: a highly successful book on Native humour, *Me Funny*, was followed by an exploration of the world of Native sexuality, called *Me Sexy*. The third instalment, on the Aboriginal creative process, called *Me Artsy*, was published this year.

His novel *Motorcycles & Sweetgrass* was published in 2010 and nominated for the Governor General's Award. Not to be outdone, 2011 saw the publication by Talonbooks of Drew's newest collection of articles and essays, *NEWS: Postcards from the Four Directions*, exploring Native existence as he sees it, in his own wonky style, followed by his two new plays, *Dead White Writer on the Floor* and *God and the Indian*. This brings his publication total to twenty-five books.

More importantly, Hayden Taylor is still desperately trying to find the time to do his laundry.

Oddly enough, the thing his mother was most proud of was his ability to make spaghetti from scratch.